The Small Things

0613-KEAR

The Small Things

A day in the life of
Brother James E. Small SJ

G. R. Kearney

0613-KEAR

Contents

This book is dedicated to my incredibly loving parents.

ACKNOWLEDGEMENTS

Father Scott Pilarz, SJ, Father William J. Byron, SJ, Father Raymond Schroth, SJ, Father Jim Gartland SJ, Cinny Green, Warren Miller, Rosa Sanchez, The Loyola Academy Community, Father Robert Ytsen, SJ, Father Norman Harland, SJ, Ted Larkin, Kathy Shinkle, The Small Family, especially Bud for all the great photographs, Pat Leydon, Antoine Howard.

To smile at someone who is sad; to visit even for a little while, someone who is lonely; to give someone shelter from the rain with our umbrella; to read for someone who is blind: these and others can be small things, very small things, but they are appropriate to give our love of God concrete expression at all.

-Mother Teresa

Foreword

Three years ago George Kearney, then a senior at Georgetown University, approached me about working with him on a writing project. It seemed a reasonable enough request, so I agreed to take it on. I did not know then that the project would change lives: George's, mine, and surely those of more than a few of its future readers. These changes can be attributed, first of all, to the nature of the study. The man who captured George's imagination, and whom George's imagination captures in this book, serves as a catalyst for the common good in the community where he works; and though his labor of love is specific to a particular school, his personal qualities and example transcend time and place. George takes the strands of one man's inconspicuous life and weaves of them a parable that challenges and consoles those of us who have never met Brother Small.

As this book makes clear, Brother Small's dedication is contagious. Certainly, George Kearney caught his spirit when he was a student at Loyola Academy, and it continues to animate him in his own work as a volunteer teacher at Cristo Rey Jesuit High School and as a writer. George has diligently worked on this manuscript with particular attention to getting details just right. His care and craftsmanship surely make his subject (and his former teacher) proud. George's work and life stand as a testimony to the man about whom he writes.

In the nineteenth-century, the Jesuit poet, Gerard Manley Hopkins, penned a tribute to a religious brother recognized for his sanctity while serving as the porter or doorman at a Jesuit house in Majorca. The poem, "In honour of St. Alphonsus Rodriguez," praises God for attending to the details of creation, such as veining violets "with trickling instrument." Hopkins argues that God's honor is "flashed off" or revealed through such small things as the petals of a flower or a simple task faithfully done. George Kearney makes the same case almost two centuries later. His tribute to Brother Small proves that the same Ignatian spirituality that inspired Rodriguez and Hopkins endures in the new millennium now dawning.

Scott Pilarz, S.J., Assistant Professor
Feast of St. Joseph the Worker, March 19, 2001
Georgetown University
Washington, D.C.

Prologue

He stormed into the kitchen, his long, curly hair framing the liquor-induced smile on his face. "Are you writing a book about Bro Small?" he practically yelled into my face. The question caught me totally off guard. I had just arrived at the Christmas party.

"Yeah, I'm gonna try to," I replied somewhat hesitantly.

"HA! I didn't believe it," he said. "In fact, I bet thirty bucks against it."

This particular reaction to the idea of me writing a book about Brother Jim Small was an entertaining one, but hardly unique. I have been working on this project for nearly two and a half years, and in that time I have been met with more half-smiles, politely surprised nods and incredulously raised eyebrows than I could ever begin to count.

When people hear that I am writing a book about a Jesuit brother, they usually say something like this: "Cool, wow, that's really cool. But, why, uhhh, I mean why'd you choose to write about this guy?"

It's an important question, because Brother Small is not brilliant. He is not rich. He is not famous. He is certainly not sexy.

Brother Small is a carpenter, janitor and artist who works in a dark, cramped and cluttered workshop deep in the basement of Loyola Academy in Wilmette, Illinois. Many people, my friend included, understand him only in the context of his simple work, his humble surroundings and his seemingly unremarkable lifestyle. As such, he hardly seems to be a suitable subject for a book.

But for a number of different reasons his life has left an indelible mark upon mine. He has pushed me to live a better life and to become a better person. His life is so remarkable, that I think it can be of service to other people.

Brother Small's way of life has been an orienting perspective for me since I met him in 1985, when I was eight years old. He volunteered to give me and another boy, Joe Fortunato, art lessons. We visited him every Sunday at Loyola for about an hour. He taught us very basic contour line drawing. I had always enjoyed drawing and I loved the art lessons. I continued to attend his informal sessions in the school library until I began high school at Loyola.

My first year there was a difficult one. I had few friends. I made the lesser of the two football teams, which in hindsight was great considering I got cut from the basketball team and the baseball team. It was a hard year because I felt I really didn't fit in anywhere, as only a pimply faced, 110-pound thirteen-year-old can.

During this time there was one place at Loyola I knew I could always go: Brother Small's workshop. The door to his cluttered quarters was always left slightly ajar, if not totally open, and the birds he kept in there could be heard singing from the remotest corners of Loyola's sprawling lower level. I dropped in to see him occasionally, and when I did, I was met with unabashed love and kindness.

"Hi G.R. Come on in. Do you have time to sit down?" Before I had uttered a word he had asked me about classes, about football, and about my parents. He listened generously as I unknowingly tried to convince myself to stay at Loyola. I didn't go in to see him too often. I felt nervous about going there. I thought people might think it was weird that I went in and visited him. So if there were other students in the hallway, I would just sidle past his door and return when the corridor was again empty.

As time wore on, and I began to feel more and more comfortable at Loyola, I visited Brother Small less and less. I did see him though, very often, making his way around the halls, smiling, greeting all of the students, fixing windows, carrying paintings or picking up garbage. He was always kind, always warm.

Eventually I graduated from Loyola and left home to attend Georgetown University in Washington, DC. During the second semester of my junior year, I studied English at King's College in London. While there, I also had an internship with William Blair L.L.C, a Chicago based, employee-owned investment banking firm. I had few responsibilities there. The office manager gave me a great deal of latitude to explore their company, their research, and as much information about the financial markets as I could find. I was then, and still am fascinated by the stock market for a number of reasons, not the least of which is the potential to make money.

If I were a cartoon character, my time at William Blair would have been best represented by my eyeballs suddenly morphing into dollar signs and spinning out of control. I didn't get paid at the internship, so I wasn't actually making any money. But, for the first time in my life, I was able to see, that I had the basic qualifications to get a job like this somewhere, and if I did, I could make a lot of cash. This was quite exciting for me. One day I overheard two of the men I worked with comparing notes on different sports cars they had both recently purchased. I figured out roughly how much those guys must've been making a year and thought about how I would spend all that money.

During January of that year, Brother Small was the subject of a brief feature on the "Today Show" on NBC. I received a copy of the show some time in February, but I couldn't get it to play on the British VCRs. So I called my sister and asked her to tell me all about it. Eventually I got the sound to play, though I wasn't able to actually watch it until I returned to the States. And with that five-minute spot on national television, Brother Small's life and values crashed headlong back into mine.

Brother Small was the perfect foil to the men and women with whom I worked at William Blair. His life revolved around God and

17

love, love for God and love for other people. Theirs appeared, at least, to revolve around money, though I feel compelled to add that this may be an unfair representation of them, as I did not know them outside of our professional setting, where it was their job to make money for other people.

Brother Small became a part of my life again at a time when, although I didn't recognize this at the time, I needed his wisdom and simplicity. I was rapidly approaching my senior year of college. The real world, which had once seemed too distant to be concerned with, loomed on the horizon. The race towards the real world would begin as soon as I returned to Georgetown. Students would begin to shuttle resumes all over the country and travel from interview to interview. It's quite possible that I would have returned to Georgetown and begun this process and the rest of my life without ever reconsidering my values and priorities, if Brother Small had not revisited me via the unyielding combo of an American tape and a British VCR.

But he did come back into my life and I found myself asking the question, why? Why would the "Today Show" feature Brother Small, a seemingly obscure janitor and artist at a Jesuit high school in Chicago? And then I began to think about his life, to analyze it in terms of other people's lives, in terms of the rest of the world. His life is different than most people's lives. His life is about love and work. It is about serving and humility. It is about generosity and the self, and denial of much that is selfish, and sometimes arguably human. His life is about being a Christian. It is, he hopes and oftentimes prays, a manifestation of his relationship with God.

As I looked forward in my life, I couldn't help but wonder if my friends at William Blair were as happy or peaceful as Brother Small. And then I couldn't help but think ahead to my life. What were my responsibilities as a Christian? What would make me happy and peaceful? How should I, if at all, try to serve other people in my life?

In the end, I decided to put the potential careers I had been considering on hold and come to Cristo Rey Jesuit High School where I have spent the last year and a half, teaching, coaching, helping lead retreats and driving a red school bus around Pilsen, a predominantly Mexican-American neighborhood on the south side of Chicago. It has been a truly joyous time, one that I couldn't even begin to explain on these pages. But I can say that I feel truly blessed to have had the opportunity to work here with the students, who are some of the most courageous and exciting people I have ever been around.

But now, as I write this, the fifth or sixth prologue to this story of Brother Small's life, I am approaching another crossroads in my life. I am five months away from completing the second year of a two-year volunteer commitment I made to Cristo Rey. It is now January of 2001. My time here will end in June. I don't really look forward to leaving. I feel a quiet but persistent unease in my gut. It is a familiar feeling, one I encountered two years ago as my time in college drew to a close. This feeling, I suspect, is linked to uncertainty about the future. I don't know what I will be doing six months from now.

As I ponder my future I very often find myself carefully calculating different people's expectations for me: my parents, my friends, my friends' parents, my parents' friends, my old teachers, my colleagues, me, and especially the students with whom I have been working.

When all is said and done, I don't know what I will do next year. I don't have any idea. I'm not even sure I know what I want to do next year. But I do know that regardless of what I choose, I will always be able to look to Brother Small's life for a very real example of how to live more compassionately, justly, generously, lovingly and selflessly. His way of life will always loom large for me as an example of how to incorporate Christian values into the potential craziness of everyday life in our world. I haven't a doubt that his life is so quietly remarkable that it can also work its way into the lives of people, who have not been blessed to know Brother Small, and gently urge them towards a better life.

And that, coupled with the fact that I believe Brother Small to be a modern-day saint, is precisely the reason why I have endeavored to write a book about him.

In the interviews I did for this book, I listened to six people tell me that they think Brother Small is a saint. He discards these comments with an air of indifference and embarrassment. "I'm not a saint. That's a crazy thing to say," Brother Small says. "I shouldn't even be mentioned in the same category as the saints. I knew a saint though. When I was down at Milford there was a Brother named Jack Kane; now he was a real true saint, but he died young. When he came into the Jesuits he was just a regular guy, but when he died a few years later he was a saint, he had become a saint."

He told me about Jack Kane, the rough-hewn redhead from the south side of Chicago. He reminisced about Jack's unyielding holiness, his probing spirituality, his constant compassion for others, his ceaseless devotion to religious life and his undying work ethic. "Oh yeah, he was a real true saint."

When I asked Brother Small how his life was any different than Jack Kane's he couldn't come up with an answer. Instead he handed me a short book, a pamphlet of sorts, titled *Brother Jack, We Need You Here!* He encouraged me to read it and told me that if I did I would be able to see why the two of them could never be put into the same category.

I read the entire thing, all eighty-some odd pages of it. In the first chapter, young Jack Kane set out uncertainly from his family's Irish enclave in Chicago for the Jesuit novitiate in Milford, Ohio. When he arrived there he made his way into the main foyer of the school where he observed the following: "A black gown filled the doorway. The young man who wore it was tall, big, broad, vast; but all frame, so that you thought of him as thin in spite of his size. The man was Brother Jim Small. With his great size, keen sense of humor, his feel for all that was human, he became Jack's closest friend and hero" (Allen, 14).

I am not at all surprised to hear that Brother Small was Brother Kane's closest friend or hero. However, at the end of *Brother Jack, We Need You Here*, I was still curious about what, if anything separated Brother Small and Brother Jack. When I asked Brother Small, he couldn't really cite anything concrete except for the fact that Brother Kane had died at an early age.

In reality, the two of them had a great deal in common. Aside from the superficial similarities, like their shared Irish heritage and neighborhood affiliations, they were both men striving to embody the Ignatian ideals of being leaders in service, contemplatives in action, and men for others. The two of them had dedicated their lives to serving other people through acts of love, kindness and hard work.

In the time since Brother Kane's death, Brother Small has remained relentlessly dedicated to these ideals. He has tried always to live them out with love, warmth and compassion towards other people. It is this simple combination, this dedication to love, which makes his life saintly.

Brother Small's life is simple. He is not a martyr; he is a carpenter. He does not work with lepers or with the poor. He lives a seemingly ordinary life, serving the relatively affluent community of Loyola Academy, a suburban college preparatory Jesuit high school.

This simplicity and ordinariness presented a dilemma for me as a writer. Initially I had tried to write a biography. I quickly found that this wasn't the best strategy. While Brother Small's life has been interesting—he grew up during the Depression, spent time in Pearl Harbor, and worked as a Chicago policeman—he has not done anything that anyone else hasn't already done, or won't do again soon. But, this doesn't change the fact that he lives so well; well enough that many people believe him to be a saint. My task as the writer has been to capture the wisdom and the values that make his life remarkable, even though they are buried in the mundane moments and events of ordinary life.

The book I have created in my attempt to accurately present Brother Small to you is a hybrid: part biography, part narrative and part reminiscence. It is a work of creative nonfiction.

Essentially the book is told through three different lenses. In the first we see Brother Small, in the present, making his way through a typical day at Loyola. In the second we see Brother Small in the past, in his youth, in his early years as a Jesuit and in his other careers. In the third we see Brother Small's life as he sees and understands it, through his own eyes, ears, thoughts, beliefs, memories and words.

The chronology of the book does not follow the events of Brother Small's life, but rather the events of his day at Loyola. We will join him when he rises early in the morning, and we will follow him through his day as he works, prays, paints, interacts with other people, eats, ministers to the sick, prays again, and finally returns to bed.

I am the narrator, but the most important sections of Brother Small's story will be told through his own words. The two of us spent countless hours in fascinating conversations that evolved out of interview questions. Fortunately I have all of these conversations on tape. They are, for me, an archive of incredible wisdom. I have tried to incorporate pieces of these conversations into the book whenever possible and appropriate.

In an effort to respect their privacy, I have occasionally changed names and altered inconsequential details about the lives of some of the players in Brother Small's day.

I hope and pray that this book may make Brother Small's life, his love, his simplicity, his peace and happiness, as accessible and meaningful for you as it has been for me. I consider myself blessed to have known him, and this is the best way I can think of to share my blessings and his life with other people.

1

Lord teach me to be generous,

Life is not made up of great
sacrifices or duties, but of little
things, of which smiles and
kindnesses and small obligations,
given habitually, are what win
and preserve the heart.

-Sir Humphrey Davy I

It is 3:52 A.M. The rest of the world is still asleep, wrapped in warm sheets and blankets when Brother James E. Small begins his day. Outside, the brilliant lights of the Edens Expressway illuminate an occasional car speeding past Loyola Academy, but there is mostly just empty pavement.

Brother Small's room in the Jesuit Residence, on the third floor of Loyola Academy is armed with three alarm clocks, each of which is set to go off at 3:55 A.M. The loudest of these clocks is situated across the room. Another substantial alarm clock sits on his nightstand. But today, like most days, he is awake before any of the alarms sound. He worries constantly that the alarms might wake some of his fellow Jesuits who live across the hall and in the adjoining rooms.

The third alarm clock is built into his watch. He often shows off this watch, which has a calculator, a phone directory and an alarm. He is particularly proud of the watch because he paid less than $7 for it.

In the darkness of the early morning, before he climbs out of bed, Brother Small bends, straightens and stretches his long skinny legs under the covers. As he lies there, he offers a quick prayer of gratitude. He doesn't feel sorry for himself because he is up early. Instead he gives thanks for his life and for the new day. Then he pulls his eighty-year-old body out of bed, slips on his glasses and begins his day by turning off his alarm clocks.

"Is time important to you, Brother Small?"

"Time is extremely important because we all have just a finite amount of it at our disposal. I try to utilize it as much as possible. Brother Haas once said that in order to get everything done we must be stingy with our time. I agree with that and I think you could say I'm very stingy with my time. Twenty-four hours a day isn't near enough time to do all of the things I want to do. Most people feel the same way."

"So, you really think you are stingy with your time?"

"Yeah, well, maybe stingy is not a good word; I guess I am appreciative of my time. There is so much to life, so much, but there is not enough time for everything, so I appreciate the time I have, because I love the things I am able to do with my time. I try not to waste the little time I have on frivolous things like worries or TV or reading novels or being angry with other people. Life is just too short to waste time on unimportant things."

Every minute of his day is important to him. He rarely says "No." In fact he always tries to say "Yes," unless something is absolutely impossible because of a lack of ability or knowledge, rather than a lack of time. He takes advantage of every single minute of his day. He has given away so much of his time that he has very little of it left for himself. So much so, that he has to rise before 4:00 a.m. in order to get everything done.

Yet, despite the fact that each of his minutes is like a nugget of gold, Brother Small manages to proceed through his days like a man with all the time in the world. He finds time to stop and talk to anyone who might want or need to talk. He can always, always make time for his visitors. Yet, the people he deals with never seem to understand that he is busy because he never shows it.

Many people can give you fifteen minutes of their time. But they spend ten of it telling you how lucky you are to have their time, and they spend the other five telling you what they *should* be doing with their time. Not Brother Small. Making people feel comfortable, happy and loved is as important to him as any of his other jobs.

Once he has climbed out of bed, he makes his way slowly across the bedroom to the adjoining bathroom. His room at Loyola is big, at least by his standards. Brother Small has not shared a room since he first joined the Jesuits. This has not been an unwelcome change because he shared a bedroom with one or two of his brothers for his entire life before joining the Jesuits.

His parents, Owen J. Small and Margaret Naughton Small, raised their six children on the far south side of Chicago, in the midst of the Great Depression. They lived in a tight bungalow at 7743 S. Hermitage in a predominantly Irish Catholic neighborhood. Today their house is gone, burned down and replaced by a parking lot, but the love and the lessons learned there live on in Jim and his surviving brothers and sisters.

Looking back on his childhood Brother Small says, "Well, I guess it was the depression and now I know that we were a little poor, but then it didn't seem so bad; it was a little tough, but we lived, didn't we?" Jim, his older sister Marge, his younger brother Jack, younger sisters Marie and Helen, and his little brother Bud, all lived under the same roof with their parents. It was not a big house. One and sometimes two of the girls slept on a daybed in the living room. The attic was converted into a bedroom for Jim and Jack. These two tall brothers shared the room and fought the cold drafty winters and dangerously low ceilings together until their family moved one block away into a considerably larger and more comfortable house. The Smalls were moving up in the world and their new house was a source of pride for all of them, especially their father. But, in less than a year, the Smalls had to give up the new place. Their father, a Chicago police officer, simply did not have the money to make payments on the new home because during much of the Depression he did not receive a paycheck on a regular basis. So, the Smalls packed up their things for the second time in a year and returned to their original cramped house on Hermitage. From that point forward, things became more and more difficult for the Smalls as their father suffered through more and more payless paydays.

He collected days old bread and bruised fruit from some of the grocery stores on his beat. The kids sprinkled scarce sugar on the stiff bread to liven it up a bit. Sometimes they had to eat orange and banana peels just to get something in their stomachs. They usually went to bed hungry, but there was very little complaining, and their father kept working throughout the entire Depression.

Growing up in the Depression has had a lasting impact on Brother Small. Despite being poor, living in a small house that was extremely hot in the summer and cold in the winter, and occasionally going to bed hungry, the Small family was happy. The six children all got along well enough. Their family ate almost every meal together. Even when the meals were nearly nonexistent, they sat down at the table together, sometimes at three in the afternoon, sometimes at nine o' clock at night, depending on when their dad returned home from his shift.

The children would clamor to the table at meal times, their faces red, their hands dirty from playing in the prairie, the vacant lot down the block from their home. Their mother prepared the food; their father, the patriarch, sat sternly at the head of the table, dictating the mood and tone of the meal with the expressions projected beneath his oft-furrowed brow.

Happiness for the eight Smalls did not rest solely on commodities or money. Their family made it through the Depression because they stuck together and depended on one another for support when their father's job was not enough.

All of the older children worked. In seventh and eighth grade Jim held down a job selling newspapers from a stand at the bustling corner of 79th street and Ashland Avenue. It was his first job, and the little money he made from his meager pay seemed great to him. Much of it was handed over to his parents, though he carefully saved every remaining cent.

In the eighth grade a new hobby attracted all of his interest and attention: photography. He had studied the camera briefly in school. It fascinated him. He converted an old coal storage room in the basement of his family's house into his own personal "dark room," where he taught himself to develop and enlarge pictures he took with a beat-up camera someone in his family had purchased years earlier.

He oftentimes paged through the newspapers he was selling, and one afternoon he came across an advertisement for Kodak cameras. He fell in love with one of the cameras and sent away for it in the spring of his eighth grade year, when he had saved up some of his money. The camera cost $13, a small fortune in 1936. But, he was able to save nearly thirty cents a week working the paper stand. He already had more than $5, and he figured if he saved all of that money he would be able to buy the camera in no time. He did worry, though, that despite his obvious earning potential the camera company would not send one of their best and most expensive cameras to a kid, so when he filled out the mail order form, Jim used his dad's name and listed his occupation as a police officer. He watched the mail for a couple weeks waiting for the bill to come, but after a while he must have forgotten about it. One Saturday morning he was fussing with his old camera in the attic when he heard his dad bellow, "JIMMMMY!" Even now his eyes light up and he flinches instinctively when he recalls his father's initial reaction to the camera invoice.

His father stood at the foot of the stairs, the bill for the camera clasped in his meaty hand. Jim began to speak halfway down the stairs, "Dad, I'm going to pay for the camera. I used your name because I didn't think they'd send it to me. I've already saved up a lot."

"You're not going to buy anything," his father grunted.

"No, I..." He began to protest but then thought better of it.

"I'll tell you what. I just got a paycheck; that's two in a row. So, I'm going to help you buy this camera," he said gruffly. "It'll be a gift for you for your graduation, okay?" He asked the question as if he expected Jim might actually say no.

"That'd be great Dad, thanks a lot." His father nodded, turned and walked away. This was certainly a pleasant surprise for Jim. By the time he graduated from Little Flower Grade School, he had a brand new Kodak camera and no bills. So, he spent all of that summer and much of his free time in high school snapping pictures around town and developing them in his basement. Even as a fourteen-year-old, he seemed to have a knack for seeing the world and, beyond that, for recording and sharing his vision and understanding.

"Were you surprised when your dad gave you the camera?"

"No. My dad was a great man and he really loved our family. He made so many sacrifices for us and he gave us so many opportunities. Our tuition for grammar school was $10 a kid. There were a couple years when we were all in school at the same time, and he had to pay $60 a year. He didn't have that kind of money because it was at the time when he wasn't collecting any money from the police department. So he asked the nuns if he could pay them as he got the extra money. He would work extra, and every time he got a few dollars here or a few dollars there, he would go straight to the school and pay off the nuns until he had paid for each one of us to be there.

I did have a tough time talking to my dad though. We weren't always that close. My dad was not proud of me at first for choosing a religious life, but eventually he came around. But even though we weren't always that close I loved him, and I learned a lot from him about my responsibilities to other people. He really was a great man."

"It seems like you had good parents. Do you have any advice for today's parents?"

"Well, parenting today is a whole lot more difficult than it was when I was a child. There wasn't a problem with dope, and alcohol didn't seem to be such a problem. There was no TV. There was only radio, and if you listened to a program you had to use your imagination, where now you just sit in front of the TV and they make it up for you.

It seems morality today is just not what it used to be. Today you have children having babies, and young people living together; and hundreds of people are having abortions everyday. But, it has become routine. We hear so much about this that we begin to think it's normal, but really values are changing and morality is being forgotten. It's not normal, yet nobody seems to notice. That puts parents in a difficult spot. In order to be a good parent, I think you must try to live a good life, a just life. If you just do the right thing your children will notice, and what you do is more important than what anyone else in the world does, because your children love you so much, and they look up to you so much."

On this cool autumn morning, Brother Small dresses quietly in the room in which he alone lives. This morning as he pulls on a pair of black trousers he gives thanks for the roof over his head and the comfortable life he is able to lead. The pants are part of his usual Jesuit outfit, and he has had this pair for six years. He also wears an old white button down dress shirt. The collar is frayed, and the right upper corner of the breast pocket has come unstitched and hangs limply. The shirt is so old that it has become transparent, and the words on his undershirt are visible: "Loyola Football '92. We will be CHAMPIONS." He wears a mismatched pair of black socks, and a well-worn pair of black shoes. Once he's dressed, he stops and rummages through the piles strewn about the top of his compact dresser. Nearly two hundred letters are stacked on the left, all of them requesting paintings. Brother Small has been working his way through the pile for three years, since he appeared on the "Today Show" in January of 1998. There are art magazines and catalogs, newspaper clippings, a few hardbound books and also a few errant tubes of paint. The trappings of the artist are very evident. He finds what he's looking for: a sealed, stamped, addressed envelope, and slides it into his pocket. He notices an envelope beneath the one he has just removed, and laughs aloud as he turns to leave the room.

He has saved the letter for seven years because it is evidence of one of his favorite pranks. Early in the fall of 1992, Stan Brietzman, a physical education teacher and baseball coach at Loyola, dropped into Brother Small's basement workshop. At the time Brother Small was using his table saw to cut various sizes of wood to use in his picture frames.

Stan said, "I took woodshop when I was in high school over at Glenbrook North, Brother Small. I can remember on the first day of class the teacher, Mr. Swagerman, his name was Harry Swagerman. He asked if there were any baseball players in the room. At the time he was explaining how the table saw worked. It looked just like the one you've got there. I raised my hand because I had played baseball for my entire life.

So he says, 'Come on up here pal.' And he had me stand in front of the class and try to catch little pieces of wood that he was dropping on the table saw. It doesn't sound hard, but they come off of there pretty quick, and you never know where they'll go for sure. Well, the whole class got a pretty good laugh because I couldn't catch any of them."

As soon as Stan left his shop that afternoon, Brother Small wrote down the name Harry Swagerman. He didn't know how he would use the name, but by Christmastime of 1993 he had formulated a plan. It all began with a sweater. "Somebody gave me a nice sweater," Brother Small says, chuckling as he remembers all of this, "but I didn't need the sweater; I had plenty of clothes." So he wrapped up the sweater and left it in Stan's mailbox with the following note. Stan would receive it on the day he returned from Christmas break.

> January 7, 1993
> Dear Stanley,
> I dropped by at your school and they told me that you were off during the holidays.
> It's been a very long time since I saw you last. I hesitate and am embarrassed to say I did time, seven years, at Attica for armed robbery; it was a "frame-up" and you know I would never do anything wrong. While serving time at Attica, my conscience bothered me and I often thought of the time I had you act like a "jumping clown," and catch wood pieces from the revolving bench saw in woodshop.
> If I can ever be of any assistance to you by coming to talk to the boys at Loyola in woodshop, let me know.

The very best to you in your carpentry and athletic career.

Sincerely yours,

Harry Swagerman

P.S. I thought you might like this sweater. It was given to
me by the warden's wife when I was released. It's not that I
don't like it, but it reminds me of that "hell-hole!"

To Brother Small's surprise and infinite pleasure, Stan bought
the story. "He believed every word of it," Brother Small says looking
back on his tomfoolery, "but when I told him, we had a great laugh."

"Is it important to have a good sense of humor in life?"

"Well, it's hard to get by without a sense of humor. You have got to
be able to laugh at all of the funny things that happen in life. It's not
good to take things too seriously. Sometimes it seems like people who
don't have a sense of humor can get depressed much easier than
those who do have a sense of humor."

"Is it important to have fun in life?"

"By all means, I think everybody has fun in different ways. For me
it means painting. I wouldn't want to paint all the time though. I have
found that just having fun or just living my life for myself is not all that
great. I think that's true. As human beings we have a tendency to live
only for ourselves, and that might mean just going out and having fun
time all the time. But if that's all life is, I think we will find it empty
and somewhat meaningless. It is more important to enjoy life. To
really enjoy it, I think the only way to do this is by following the Commandments. That might not be 'fun,' but it will help us to a deeper
enjoyment of life."

Kindness and a good sense of humor are never far apart. Brother
Small is living proof of this. He has a gift for making people laugh
without harming anyone. He has a generous sense of humor, one that
everyone can enjoy. Beyond that, he has a great sense of theatrics.

In 1990, Beth Scully—who was then the director of Loyola's
O'Shaughnessy Program, a support system for freshmen students

with above average intelligence but slight deficits in the reading and language areas—was planning a garage sale in her nearby Northfield home. She was anxious about a group of transient gypsies who were suspected of committing small-scale burglaries and thefts in and around her neighborhood.

"Bro, I don't know, I just don't want anybody to come walking into my garage, or worse my house and stealing, especially the stuff I am not trying to sell."

Her concerns about the garage sale got Brother Small's wheels spinning. By Saturday, the day of the sale, he had procured a blonde wig, and a battered trench coat. He had also arranged to borrow a sizable but elderly Buick from one of his friends who lived close to the school.

He pulled up in front of the Scully residence minutes after Beth had opened her garage door on that Saturday morning. She and her friends turned and looked as the long sky blue Buick rolled to a conspicuous stop in front of the house. They saw a large man with long curly blonde hair lower the passenger window and turn to address them.

"Who in the world is this?" one of them wondered aloud before he began to speak.

"WHAT TIME OPEN?" He waited for a moment and then yelled it again at the top of his lungs, "WHAT TIME OPEN?" He waited and yelled again, "WHAT TIME OPEN?"

"We're already open," Beth shouted back.

"Okay, I go get my boys. Be right back."

He pulled away. Those in the driveway were dumbstruck. Beth didn't know who the man was, but she had a feeling that he and his blue Buick were not a part of any thieving troop of gypsies. But, she did wonder uneasily if he and his friends would in fact return. Whether or not he was a gypsy, she did not want him or any of his buddies returning to her garage.

He didn't return, and when he saw her in school Monday morning, he could barely contain himself. As soon as he saw her, he started laughing but managed to say, "What time open?"

Beth pieced it together immediately. She recalls, "The two of us stood in the hall and laughed like crazy. For fifteen years he kept me laughing. Every time I saw him he had a joke or a funny story or, even better, a practical joke. He is a riot. But his humor is motivated by kindness and that is what makes it so special."

He opens the heavy wooden door and leaves his room chuckling quietly about the letter to Stan. He walks down the attractively carpeted dimly lit hallway towards the small chapel in the Jesuit residence. On his way out he passes his reflection in the window, but he does not so much as glance at it; he just walks past, with his head bent slightly forward. His external appearance seems to hardly concern him at all anymore.

Throughout his entire morning routine, he tries to pray or, at least, to think about the prayers he will say later in the day. He says, "If I start thinking about all of the things I have to do during the day as soon as I get out of bed, I'll lose control of my thoughts, and those things will end up controlling my thoughts and my prayers will become very difficult." He recognizes the difference between his needs and the things he needs to do. He balances his life by separating the two.

It is just one minute past four in the morning when Brother Small enters the chapel. At this time most of the Loyola community, and probably all of the students, are sleeping soundly in their homes, which are scattered around Chicago and its north suburbs. Many of these people are already a part of Brother Small's life, and some of them will become part of his life on this particular day.

One of these people, Melanie Selva, a Loyola junior rolls over in her narrow twin bed and awakens with a start. She sits up and looks around the room. Her roommate, Laura Sims is sleeping soundly on the other side of the room. She realizes where she is, relaxes and eases herself back down into the bed, pulling the covers up around her neck. She glances across the room as she tries to once again get comfortable in her bed. Pockets of light from a yellow street lamp sneak through the tree next to her bedroom window and dance across the pictures of her father, brother and grandmother that hang on the wall immediately above her desk. Then her eyelids drop slowly and she drifts again into an uneasy sleep.

A couple of miles north and a few blocks east of Loyola, in the suburb of Winnetka, Patrick Martin, a Loyola junior, sleeps in the guestroom at his good friend and soccer teammate Mike McDermott's expansive suburban home.

Blocks away, Timothy Ryan lies next to his wife Lynne, an hour and a half away from the call of the morning alarm and the beginning of another day of work for one of the country's largest financial services corporations. But now they sleep soundly in a king-sized bed filled with pillows and covered with a luxurious, lavishly decorated comforter.

In Evanston, a nearby town, Father Norman Harland SJ struggles to fall back to sleep amidst the constant drone of machines in the cool clean hospital room tucked high in the northeast corner of the sprawling Evanston Hospital building. This has been his home for the past month and a half as he has battled cancer of the stomach and esophagus.

The chapel is dark and quiet when Brother Small enters. He leaves the overhead light off and cautiously makes his way around the chairs and across the chapel to the far corner where the tabernacle sits on a table. A small red light always burns in the corner of the room above the tabernacle. Brother Small kneels on the ground before the dim red light and the plain wooden box. He does not say anything. He is still. His eyes are closed, his head bowed and his surprisingly strong hands are still, folded in front of him.

Behind the closed door of the tabernacle sits a plate filled with unleavened bread, the physical element of the Catholic sacrament of the Eucharist. The bread, which has been blessed or consecrated by a priest, is understood to be the physical presence of Christ. Each morning Brother Small gets up and visits the Blessed Sacrament, the presence of Christ. As a Christian and a Jesuit, Brother Small strives to emulate Christ in everything he does, and visiting the Blessed Sacrament in the morning reminds him why he has chosen to be a Jesuit and how important his work as a Jesuit really is. It helps him to focus on the ways he can follow Christ in the simple activities that make up his day.

He opens his eyes, and gazes for a moment upon the tabernacle. The red light reflects off the thick lenses of his glasses. Then he rises slowly and quietly leaves the chapel with his head bowed.

Once he's done with his morning visit to the Blessed Sacrament, Brother Small walks out of the chapel and into the kitchen where he pours himself a cup of coffee. Then he takes the elevator down from the Jesuit residence to the first floor where he begins his morning chores. He walks through the administrative hallway to the back doors of the school. He unlocks and opens the door, gazing out into the dark quadrangle and parking lot. He sees his breath floating in the air. He smells autumn as the wind blows through the quad and scatters a pile of leaves still damp with the morning dew. He watches with a smile as a small robin pulls a worm out of the soft ground beneath a tree near the door. He has stopped for just a few seconds, and he turns again towards the school.

Once he's unlocked the door, he turns and heads the other direction down the hallway. As he walks slowly through the administrative corridor, a car passes the school on Laramie Avenue and some light from the headlights of the car somehow makes its way into the school building where it ghosts across the collection of class pictures that hang in the administrative hallway. In that moment, Brother Small sees the faces of two or three of the boys who graduated from Loyola some years ago. The faces in the picture look a lot like his high-school face, which hangs in a similar picture on a wall in another Catholic school on the south side of the city.

He attended St. Rita High, a Catholic high school run by Augustinian Priests. At that time in his life, Jim Small hoped to someday become a priest. He'd wanted to become a priest since the sixth grade when he heard two missionary priests speak about their work. Today he can't remember their names or the location of their missions. He does, however, acknowledge that they first inspired him to a life of service. Something attracted him to their simple lives of service work. Jim's life as a priest never came to fruition because he could not speak or understand Latin, the language of the Catholic mass at that time. So once he got into high school he set his sights on the brotherhood instead.

Most religious orders have both brothers and priests, although brothers are becoming more and more rare. Priests and religious brothers have much in common. Externally they are almost indistinguishable. Jesuit priests and Jesuit brothers usually wear black shirts and black slacks. The priests wear a solid white collar around their necks. The brothers wear the same outfit, but their collars are slightly different; they are white like the priests, but there is a small pie shaped piece taken out of the bottom of the brothers' collars.

Aside from the one difference in their external appearances, priests and brothers do have different responsibilities in the church and the Society. First of all, brothers cannot say mass, or perform most Catholic sacraments. Priests can. As a result, the two groups are trained somewhat differently.

When a man enters the Society of Jesus, the religious order more commonly referred to as the Jesuits, he chooses to become either a priest or a brother. If he chooses to become a priest, he must study and prepare for twelve years. He begins as a novice. Then, he works and studies as a scholastic until he is ordained a priest. If, however, he decides to become a brother, he becomes a brother immediately. When Brother Small entered the society, the training for the Jesuit Brothers was more vocational than the arduous intellectual training required for the scholastics. At that time, Jesuit brothers were trained in a specific skill, like carpentry, cooking, medicine or plumbing. The vocational training helped the Jesuit communities around the country function as almost totally self-sufficient organizations. Fifty years ago, every Jesuit community had nearly equal numbers of priests and brothers. Today, Jesuit communities are lucky if they have one brother, and more often than not, that one brother is an old school figure who is nearing the end of his active career in the Society of Jesus.

When the Augustinian Priests at St. Rita learned of Jim's interest in a religious vocation they began counseling him and directing him in his decision. A young priest by the name of Father Lynn assumed this responsibility and counseled Jim about religious life. Soon after they met, Jim told Father Lynn that he would enter the Augustinian order as soon as he graduated from high school. At the beginning of his senior year, Fr. Lynn, however, was called away to Europe and Jim was left to ponder his future alone. He was still interested in religious life, but Father Lynn's departure planted a seed of doubt in his mind about his future with the Augustinian Order.

In April of his senior year, Jim, having heard nothing from Father Lynn or any of his Augustinian colleagues, gave up and contacted his cousin, Fr. Joe Small, a Jesuit. At this time Joe Small was a Jesuit scholastic. Jim spoke to him and decided that he would apply to the Jesuits instead of the Augustinians. As soon as he graduated, he did so and was accepted. He told his family he had decided to enter the Jesuits. His older sister Marge and his mother cried at the thought of him leaving home. His dad questioned his decision.

"Are you sure you don't want to work on the force?"

"Dad, I've wanted to do this for a long time. I think this is what I am meant to be doing. I just have this feeling, you know, I am just really interested in a religious life. I'm not sure why exactly, but I know I want to do it."

"But Jimmy, the Jesuits? They're all scholars, if you're going to be a Jesuit you're going to have to do more school and read a lot of books. They're kind of a snooty bunch you know? I mean what's wrong with being an Augustinian brother?"

"I talked to Joe, and he told me a lot of great things about the

Jesuits. I think I'll really like them, and I won't have to do as much studying as you think. The life of a brother is a lot different than the life of a priest. They study a lot, Latin, theology and all that. The brothers do more work. I'll have to go to classes, but mostly vocational classes, like my shop classes at St. Rita, and then I'll do work like that for the order."

"I still think you'd like police work more," his father concluded gruffly. Jim's grandfather had been a policeman, and his father had followed in his footsteps. He had always thought Jim, his first son would be a policeman too; it made sense. He had looked forward to working with his son. The realization that this dream would not come true was a painful one.

Jim's initial experience with the Jesuits could have been better. As soon as he arrived at the Jesuit novitiate in Milford, Ohio, he felt lonely. There was a large group of novice and brother novices there, and a senior priest was assigned to work with all of the new Jesuits. But this priest focused most all of his energy and attention on a retreat he had been preparing for the novices. As a result, the new brother novices were left on their own with very little direction from their superiors. The scholastics and brothers spent very little time together. In his time at Milford, Jim was afforded the opportunity to speak to the scholastics only on rare occasions.

After a few months, Jim could no longer take the loneliness. He was, quite simply, miserable with religious life. He left the Jesuit novitiate at Milford and took the train back to Chicago.

Once he was back in Chicago, he called home. His sister Marge answered the phone and spoke to him briefly. Surprised, she hung up the phone and said, "Jimmy's home. He left the Jesuits. He needs a ride; he's down at the Illinois Central Station at 63rd & Woodlawn." As soon as Mr. Small heard this, he slammed his hand against the table. "I knew it!" he said. "I told you he wouldn't last more than six months, and he barely lasted three. He can't make up his mind to stay in the same place for more than a couple weeks. Now he's probably got some cock-eyed plan to be a photographer or a racecar driver. You never know with him. Someday he'll figure it out and join the police force. He could do so much with his life but he doesn't know where to begin."

Brother Small continues past the class pictures, which are once again shrouded in darkness now that the car has passed the school and continued down Laramie Avenue. His second chore this morning is to open the library for Ted Larkin, the Boys Hope Girls Hope coordinator, who has a large meeting at 7:00 A.M. At that time of the morning, most of the doors in the school would still be locked, so last night Mr. Larkin asked Brother Small if he would open them. "Sure, sure Ted, we'll do it for you," Brother Small replied.

"You can ask him to do something," comments Larkin, "and he says 'Okay, we'll do that.' He doesn't write it down or anything, but you know he'll do it, he'll do it soon, and it will be done perfectly. He is a professional, and he takes great pride in his work no matter what he is doing."

Mr. Larkin once asked Brother Small to hang some pictures and a bulletin board in the Boys Hope Girls Hope office in the basement of the school.

"I talked to him about it on a Tuesday, sometime in the morning. We all left around five-thirty that night, and we locked up the doors. When I opened up the office at seven-thirty next morning, the two pictures and the bulletin board were all hanging exactly where I'd asked him to put them. You can always depend on him."

Larkin adds the following statement that captures perfectly Brother Small's value as an employee at Loyola, as a Jesuit, but most importantly, as a person, "Most of us are nice people, but we muck up once in a while. Fifty per cent of the time, we're perfect; twenty-five per cent of the time we do pretty well; but we let the other twenty-five per cent fall off the table. He's not like that though, one hundred per cent of the time it's perfect. I've never heard of him making a mistake. You ask him to do something, and it's done; you don't ever have to think about it again."

Brother Small unlocks the doors, disables the alarm, and heads for the Jesuit residence. On his way back he passes through the main foyer of the school. He ducks his head into the small office behind the receptionist's desk at the front of the school and reaches into his pocket. He pulls out the envelope and sets it into the outgoing mail basket.

The envelope contains a letter he has just completed. He is not a particularly fast typist; it took him three days to write and type the letter in one of the school's computer labs. He is going to send it to one of his old art students. He and this young woman, Margaret, a junior at Miami University in Ohio have not only kept in touch, but also, have become great friends since she stopped taking art lessons seven years ago. She is presently studying and traveling for a semester in Alaska.

Dear Margaret;

I received your postcard from the top of the world. I can't believe that you only get one hour of night each day (or I should say each night). I was so happy to hear from you and to know you are safe and sound. I can't wait to see you again and to hear all about your trip. It will be good to see the pictures you did take and the ones you will take before you leave for home.

Margaret dear, I read a very good story recently in a book called *Chicken Soup for the Christian Soul*, and I would like to tell you about it. For three days a fierce winter storm had traveled 1,500 miles across the North Pacific from Alaska, packing gale force winds and torrential rains. In the Sierra Nevadas to the east, the snow was piling up and would offer great skiing once the storm had passed.

In the foothills of the Sierras, in the town of Grass Valley, California, the streets were flooded, and in some parts of town, the power was off where trees had blown down. At the small church, the heavy rain and high winds beat against the windows with a violence that Father O'Malley had never before heard.

In his tiny bedroom, Father O'Malley was laboriously writing Sunday's sermon by candlelight. Out of the darkness, the phone in his office rang, shattering his concentration. He picked up the candle and with his hand cupped in front of it, ambled down the hall in a sphere of dim flickering light.

As he picked up the phone, a voice quickly asked, "Is this Father O'Malley?"

"Yes."

"I'm calling from a hospital in Auburn," said a concerned female voice. "We have a terminally ill patient who is asking us to get someone to give him the last rites of the Church. Can you come quickly?"

"I'll try my best to make it," Father O'Malley answered, "but, the river is over its banks and the trees are blown down all over town. It's the worst storm I've seen in all the years I've been here. Look for me within two hours."

The trip was only thirty miles, but it would be hard going. The headlights on Father O'Malley's twenty-year old car barely penetrated the slashing rain, and where the winding road crossed and recrossed the river in a series of small bridges, trees had blown down over the river's banks. But for some reason there was always just enough room for Father O'Malley to make his way around them. His progress was slow and cautious, but he continued onward to the hospital.

Not a single vehicle passed him during his long, tense journey. It was way past midnight and anyone else out on a night like this would also have to be on an emergency mission.

Finally in the near distance, the lights of the small hospital served as a beacon to guide Father O'Malley for the last 500 yards, and he hoped he had arrived in time. He parked

behind the three other cars in the parking lot to avoid as
much of the wind as possible, slipped into the right hand seat
and awkwardly wrestled his way into his raincoat before step-
ping out into the wind-whipped deluge.

With his tattered Bible tucked deep inside his overcoat
pocket, Father O'Malley forced the car door open, stepped
out and then leaned into the wind. Its power almost bowled
him over, and he was nearly blown away from the hospital
entrance.

Once inside, the wind slammed the hospital door shut
behind him, and as he was shaking the water from his coat,
he heard footsteps headed his way. It was the night nurse.

"I'm so glad you could get here," she said. "The man I
called you about is slipping fast, but he is still coherent. He's
been an alcoholic for years, and his liver has finally given out.
He's been here for a couple of weeks this time, and he hasn't
had a single visitor. He lives up in the woods, and no one
around here knows much about him. He always pays his bills
with cash and doesn't seem to talk much. We've been treat-
ing him off and on for the last couple years but this time it's
as though he's reached some personal decision and given up
the fight."

"What's your patient's name?" Father asked.

"The hospital staff has just been calling him Tom," she
replied.

In the soft night light of the room, Tom's thin sallow
countenance looked ghostlike behind a scraggly beard. It
was as though he had stepped over the threshold and his life
was already gone.

"Hello Tom. I'm Father O'Malley. I was passing by and I
thought we could talk a bit before you go to sleep for the
night."

"Don't give me that line," Tom replied. "You didn't just
stop by at 3:30 in the morning. I asked the nurse to call a

priest to give me the last rites of the Church because I know I'm about finished and about to die." Father O'Malley began to say the prayers for the last rites.

After the "Amen," Tom perked up a bit, and he seemed to want to talk.

"Would you like to make a confession?" Father O'Malley asked him.

"Absolutely not," Tom answered. "But I would like to just talk before I go."

And so Tom and Father O'Malley talked about the Korean War and the ferocity of the winter storm, and the knee-high grass and summer blossoms that would soon follow.

Occasionally during the hour or so before daylight, Father O'Malley would ask Tom again, "Are you sure you don't want to confess anything?"

After a couple of hours, and after the fourth or fifth time that Father O'Malley asked the same question, Tom replied, "Father, when I was young, I did something that was so bad that I haven't spent a single day since without thinking about it and reliving the horror."

"Don't you think it would be good for you to tell me about it?" Father asked.

"Even now, I still can't talk about what I did," Tom said, "even to you."

But as the gray light of dawn crept into the room and began to form shadows, Tom sadly said, "Okay. It's too late for anyone to do anything to me now, so I guess I might as well tell you.

I worked as a switchman on the railroad all my life, until I retired a few years ago and moved up here to the woods. Thirty-two years, two months and eleven days ago, I was working in Bakersfield on a night kind of like tonight."

Tom's face became intense as the words began to tumble out. "It happened during a bad winter storm with a lot of rain,

50 mile-an-hour winds and almost no visibility. It was two nights before Christmas, and to push away the gloom, the whole yard crew drank all through the swing shift. I was drunker than the rest of them, so I volunteered to go out in the rain and wind and push the switch for the northbound 8:30 freight."

Tom's voice dropped almost to a whisper as he went on. "I guess I was more drunk than I thought I was because I pushed that switch in the wrong direction. At 45 miles an hour that freight train slammed into a passenger car at the next crossing and killed a young man, his wife and their two daughters."

"I have had to live with my being the cause of their deaths every day since then."

There was a long moment of silence as Tom's confession of this tragedy hung in the air. After what seemed like an eternity, Father O'Malley gently put his hand on Tom's shoulder and said very quietly, "If I can forgive you, God can surely forgive you Tom, because in that car were my mother, my father and my two sisters" (Canfield, Hansen, Aubrey, Mitchell & Miller, 6-10).

With that story I'll close for now, Margaret. I love you very much and miss you. You and the whole group are in my prayers each and every day. Take good care of yourself

With Love always,

Bro. Jim

PS. Overlook the mistakes.

After he drops the letter in the mailbox at the school switchboard, Brother Small heads back up to the Jesuit residence where he refills his coffee and retires to his room. Armed with an hourglass and a fresh cup of coffee, he sits down to begin his hour-long morning prayer session. Even for him it is not always easy to sit and pray for an hour, but he takes his spirituality seriously. He prays when he is tired,

when he is bored and when he is sick. He uses the hour from 4:30 to
5:30 a.m. to reflect on many different things: God, relationships, sin,
work, and how best to live in the coming day. In the morning he always
prays on certain ideas and points that he has chosen the night before.

The hourglass, a gift from his close friend Brother Bill Haas SJ,
has become an important element of his prayer. It keeps the time, but
more importantly, the hourglass inspires him. Brother Haas knew of
Brother Small's affinity for St. Teresa of Avila. St. Teresa, one of the
great Catholic saints, used to shake her hourglass violently so as to
speed up the time she spent praying. Brother Small takes solace in
the fact that prayer has been difficult even for the greatest of the
saints.

An hourglass is still an hourglass, though, and shaking it does not
make it easier to get through an hour of prayer. That story, however,
inspires Brother Small to pray; even when it is difficult, he knows it is
absolutely necessary.

Prayer is preparation and proper preparation requires dedication. Each morning when Brother Small prays, he is preparing for his
work and for his life. Preparation is a necessary and central ingredi-
ent for success in any endeavor, whether it is painting, football, academics or business. Brother Small approaches his prayer schedule
and responsibilities as a Jesuit with tremendous dedication and discipline. His life's work is basically to imitate Christ. This is, needless
to say, a daunting task and a challenging way of life.

Yet Brother Small seems to succeed in his life's work, and he
attributes his ability to do so to prayer.

"Prayer is like gassing up the car in the morning," he says. "You do
it so that you can run all day; if you don't do it, you just can't go
anywhere, you can't do anything. Prayer gives the things and events in
my life purpose and meaning."

He begins this morning's prayer session with an exercise called
the First Prelude. This title, which comes from St. Ignatius' *Spiritual
Exercises*, is really just a fancy way of saying "pick a place." In the First
Prelude, Brother Small picks a place. It can be any place. Sometimes

he picks the Crucifixion of Jesus. Then he visualizes the cross and Jesus nailed to the cross right before his eyes. Sometimes he picks the crib of a newborn. He stands and watches the child, lost in the wonder of life. He bends down to the side of the crib reaching in and touching the baby's face. The child smiles and giggles. Brother Small sees God in the baby's smile. "God must have taught that baby to smile. How else would a tiny little baby know how to do something so beautiful and perfect?"

On this particular day, he thinks of a place in the northern suburbs of Chicago. He keeps thinking until he can picture a room in someone's home. He sees himself sitting alone by the window in this person's home. Sunlight floods into the room through the window. The light is so bright that it illuminates the tiny dust particles floating in the air. Brother Small visualizes the room and then visualizes the sparks in the sun floating before his eyes.

He uses the First Prelude as a way to slow down and take himself out of the hustle and bustle of day-to-day life. By putting himself in a peaceful place or a place of great significance to him, he is able to gain perspective on his life. He can forget for a moment his chores for the day, the painting he must finish, the pictures he must frame and the hospital he must visit. For an hour, early in the morning, he takes the time to focus on who he is, rather than what he must do in the coming day.

Once he's completed the First Prelude, he begins the Second Prelude. In this section, he prays for his needs and desires, for other people's needs, and also in thanksgiving for all that he has been given. Today he prays for seventeen different things. All of the following are included. He prays

For the grace of prayer;

For recollection of moments passed, both good and bad;

For trust in God and other people;

In thanksgiving for all that God has done for him.

In thanksgiving for angels;

> In thanksgiving for all God has done for all of humankind;
> That God will help him recognize his faults;
> That God will help him to get rid of his faults and live a
> more selfless and noble life;
> In thanksgiving for the gift of prayer;
> For the strength of the church;
> For humankind.

He makes numerous prayers. Some are personal; others are universal. He prays for individuals, for his sins, for his faults, for forgiveness, for strength. His prayer amazes me. I can't help but think that I would be a much better person if I could dedicate some of my time to thinking about other people, their needs, desires and problems. I would probably think of others before myself sometimes. I might even act more often out of concern for the well being of other people. If I spent an hour each day praying with God, I would probably be able to see how God is working in my life. I have tried but I find it difficult, and I struggle to approach this part of my life with any real discipline.

Once he has finished the Second Prelude, Brother Small begins praying on his points. Occasionally he has three or even four points for his morning prayer, but today like most days, there is only one point. He wrote it down along with all of the information for the First and Second Preludes last night. The one point for this morning's prayer comes from a book called *Cloud of Unknowing*, by an unknown author. Brother Small has scrawled the point into his prayer book. In nearly indecipherable black print it says: "This exercise cannot be achieved by intellectual labor alone."

The "exercise" referred to by Brother Small is the central idea in *Cloud of Unknowing*. It consists of the understanding that God is alive and working within each and every one of our lives.

Brother Small and I discussed this particular point later.

"Do you understand what it means?" he asked me.

"Sure," I replied. "It means you can't do this exercise with your mind . . . with your intellect; you need more, right?"

"Well, do you know what the exercise is?" he asked.

"No, I don't really have any idea," I confessed. Then he went on to explain it, by saying essentially that God is in fact alive in each of us and playing a role in our lives whether or not we know it.

Then he continued, "If you can't do it with intellectual labor, what are you supposed to use?"

I remained silent because I didn't know.

"Love," he said. "It's gained by love not by intellectual labor."

He went on to explain how this worked. "Well, you've got preachers all over the world in all kinds of different churches. All of these preachers do a lot of good things, but sometimes you'll see they take credit for all the good that happens. Well, none of us know for sure why any of that happens. You might have a little old lady in the back of the church who has a great big heart, and she is concerned for a lot of people in a lot of places. Well, maybe she really prays for them. She asks God to look over them and guard them and she tells God that she loves them. Her prayer is just as important as the work of the greatest theologians and preachers because it is motivated by love, and that is the only thing that can really make a difference. In order to know God and to understand the ways God works in our lives, we must first develop a deep true love and respect for God, then love and respect for other people will come easy."

Much of Brother Small's busy morning is spent in prayer. But this break in the activity does not bother him. He gives up this time to give himself to the Lord so that he may be able to better give love and kindness to the people he will serve on this day.

Oftentimes we define generosity in terms of dropping money in the basket. Generosity for Brother Small is radically different; it is a way of life. He spends his days giving himself to other people, serving other people and loving other people. This is his job and his calling as a Christian and a Jesuit. In fact, St. Ignatius, founder of the Jesuits, prayed time and time again, "Lord, teach me to be generous."

Brother Small spends this morning preparing to do that, praying that he may be more generous, that he may give more and that somehow he may love more.

2

Teach me to serve you as you deserve

It is amazing what God can
accomplish through an imperfect
person who has put all his
imperfections completely at
God's disposal.

-Anonymous

It is now 5:30 A.M. With his morning prayer complete, Brother Small sets his mind to painting. He heads to his studio, which is located on the second floor, just below his third floor bedroom. He turns on the light in his studio and reaches for his glasses, an old pair of women's reading glasses. Many years ago, he bought the big awkward looking spectacles with red translucent frames at a local pharmacy. They are not just reading glasses; they are actually magnifying glasses. Brother Small says these goofy looking octagonal lenses help him see the minutest details of the master works he oftentimes copies. They also help him see the intricacies of his own work, the ones that would escape his normal vision. As long as they do that, he sees no reason to replace them. It's amazing that he can use these bulky, oversized women's glasses to hone in on the tiniest details in his paintings without ever losing sight of the larger picture he is working to create. He is able to immerse himself in the small things without ever losing sight of the beauty and importance of the big picture.

He sits down and studies the little bit of work he has already completed. So far he has painted a white wooden rowboat right in the middle of the canvas. It is surrounded by sand, the beginning of a beach, and the bodies of two people, one sitting and one standing against the boat. A poster of the same scene hangs just above and to the left of his easel. He studies it for a moment and then reaches for a paintbrush and begins to paint.

Jim Small has been interested in art since grade school. He has always loved working with his hands, whether it was building birdhouses, developing photographs in a homemade dark room or drawing. As a child he never sat still. He had many hobbies, and they were always changing. He would begin with one, pursue it with passion until he discovered another one he liked better, and then he would drop everything and pursue his new hobby with even greater vigor and dedication.

In his sixth year at the Little Flower grade school, Jim got a chance to showcase one of his hobbies in school. Sister Vivian, Jim's sixth grade teacher had assigned a drawing project, and each student was expected to produce a piece of art. Jim had chosen to draw a seascape with three boats. The drawing turned out quite well. He had been so excited about the project that he had taken it home so that he could spend more of his time working on it.

On the due date, Sister Vivian made her way around the room slowly picking up each of the drawings. She moved gracefully in her floor length black gown and lily-white habit, pausing for a moment to study each drawing as she gathered it in, and then offering some brief words of congratulations. When she collected Jim's drawing, she stopped and stared at it, silenced for a moment by the quality of the work. "Outstanding," she said while the hard features of her young face softened into a smile. "Jim, this is outstanding."

The drawing was seemingly flawless. Jim had fashioned the three sailboats with incredible attention to detail. They must have been copied from somewhere, because there were so many details: weathered ropes, hanging nets, tall masts, frayed sails, and such realistic figures standing watch on the decks of the various boats. Without telling him, Sister Vivian took the picture up to St. Xavier's College, which was, at the time, located at 49th and Cottage Grove.

She took the picture to an old friend of hers, a Mercy nun who had been working and living at the college for years. "I have a drawing here one of my students did. It's really quite good, and if I remember correctly, this is the time of year for your art contest."

"Yes, the contest is next week."

"Well, is there any way we can enter this drawing?"

"I don't see why not," her friend replied. That settled it; Jim's picture would have a chance to compete against the work of about twenty college-age artists. A week later, when Sister Vivian handed the projects back, she told Jim what she had done with his drawing and encouraged him to go down to the school and see how it had fared in the art competition.

The next day after school, Jim paid seven cents to take the street-car to St. Xavier's. He went by himself and didn't tell anyone he was going. He had never in his life been that far north. He followed Sister Vivian's directions to the school. When he found it, he made his way past a large wooden door and entered a pristine world of long silent hallways and dark wood. He wandered aimlessly, soaking in the smells and sights. He gazed up at the high vaulted ceilings, and glanced into each of the recessed doorways. He wondered what could be behind the big wooden doors. He walked slowly and quietly; he was taken aback by the silence that prevailed at the school. Then he stumbled upon his drawing, hanging high on the wall above a bunch of other drawings. There was a blue ribbon hanging beneath his picture. Second place. His name was written on a piece of paper beneath the drawing. His picture was hanging between the first and third place winners. There were at least twenty other pictures hanging below his.

He looked for someone who might be able to tell him when he could pick up his drawing. "Excuse me, Sister," he said to a tall, dour looking nun who was making her way quickly but quietly down the hall. "Do you know when we can get our pictures back?" She looked surprised.

"Is one of these pictures yours?" she asked.

"Uh, yes, the one there with the boats is mine," Jim said hastily as he pointed to his picture.

"That's your picture?" she said, clearly doubting that this grade schooler had produced a drawing capable of winning an art contest for college students.

"Yes, its mine."

"What is your name, young man?"

"I'm Jim Small."

"Well, I guess you can have your picture right now," she said somewhat reluctantly. "I think they were planning on taking them down tomorrow." She reached up and took the picture off the wall and handed it to him.

"Thank you, Sister."

"You're welcome," she said, "and, well, congratulations." She handed him the ribbon.

"Thanks, Sister," he said as he wrapped up the picture and then folded up the ribbon and put it in the back pocket of his trousers. When he got home, he told his family. "Look what I did today," he said as he unwrapped his drawing and laid it on the dining room table. "I entered an art contest down at St. Xavier's. Well, I didn't really enter. Sister Vivian took my drawing down there and entered it in the contest for me."

He was excited, and he dug into the back pocket of his pants and pulled out the ribbon. "It was this drawing here that I did for school. And I won. See this ribbon; see it, Margie, I came in second place." He was thrilled, but nobody seemed to care. His father sat in his chair across the room. He looked up over his reading glasses and asked, "What are you doing? Some kind of art? Jimmy, art won't get you anywhere; drawing, painting, that stuff is for the birds. You stick to your books, and you'll be just fine."

"I think it's a nice drawing, Jim," his mom said, as she looked the drawing over quickly, "but don't leave it here because we're going to eat soon." She patted his shoulder and in a moment she was gone, back in the kitchen preparing dinner. No one encouraged him to hang it up. No one offered to get it framed. He looked around the room before he took the drawing up to the attic. His sister Marge was still gazing at the drawing. His brother Jack had lost interest. His father had his nose buried in the newspaper and his mom was in the kitchen. Jim wrapped up his drawing again and put it away in the closet he shared with his brother. He never mentioned it again; neither did anyone else.

Looking back sixty-nine years later, Marge says, "He didn't get much encouragement from home when it came to his artwork; our father wanted him to be a police officer, but that didn't stop him. He really loved his art, and I think he knew he was good at it." Despite the fact that no one ever really supported Jim's artistic pursuit, he stuck with it and took a couple of art and drafting classes in high school. Since then, it has remained his favorite hobby.

His art has become more meaningful since he joined the Jesuits. Now, it is more than a pleasant avocation, it is also an expression of the central tenets of his distinctively Jesuit spirituality. First and foremost, art is a beautiful way for Brother Small to work for the greater glory of God. This idea, working for God's glory and honor, is at the center of Jesuit life, work and spirituality. Brother Small does not paint just because he enjoys doing it. He paints to serve God and to serve other people.

Beyond that, artists have the ability to help others see. Painters paint with the goal that others will see and appreciate their work. In that sense, they control what others see. Many Jesuit artists have used their art to help others see God. They have painted everything, not just religious paintings, but when they paint, they paint with God in mind. In that way, they are able to help others see God in normal everyday events and scenes.

In his essay "Art and the Spirit of the Society of Jesus," the late Father Pedro Arrupe, the Superior General of the Jesuits, says, "St. Ignatius would tell us, the earth, like the heavens, narrates the glory of God. The average man however, is both a poor viewer and a poor narrator. Therefore he needs the artist to direct his view and to speak for him" (87).

Jesuit artists use their work to help elevate men and women to

God. They use art as a way to bring people to the fullness of Christ, but they do this without creating explicitly Christian art. As Father Arrupe says in his essay, "I do not mean that our themes have necessarily to be Christian; I mean that, whatever our theme, Christ should be its inspiration and goal" (89).

Lastly, art serves as an important channel between experience and spirituality. Art can bring beauty to prayer and life. A spiritual life without appreciation or at least recognition of the truth of human experience would be empty if not useless. Brother Small's art couples beauty, God and real world experience. Most importantly the art leads others to these very things as Robert Browning said,

> If you get simple beauty and nought else,
> You get about the best thing God invents:
> That's somewhat: and you'll find the soul you
> have missed,
> Within yourself, when you return him thanks (qtd. in Arrupe 89).

"Is your art a spiritual experience for you, Brother Small?"

"Yes, definitely, just walking into my studio and beginning to work on my paintings brings a certain peace to my soul. I enjoy painting and listening to the classical music on the radio at the same time, and it is a peaceful experience. Time goes by extremely fast when I'm in there and that's one way to tell if you are doing a good thing, whenever time goes by fast, it shows you are enjoying it.

My work also becomes a spiritual experience because I know I am doing it, not just because I love to do it, but for the glory of God and for the benefit of other people. Any work, no matter how mundane it is, can become a spiritual experience if we do it for the love of God and not just for personal benefit. I wouldn't enjoy my paintings nearly as much if I just painted for myself."

It is now ten minutes to seven and, after an hour and a half of non-stop painting, Brother Small dips the three brushes he has been using this morning into the jar of turpentine which rests on the right side of his easel. He rinses them off in the grimy sink on the opposite side of the room. He sets his glasses down on the table and then puts the brushes back in the rack with the other fifty or so brushes in his studio. He meticulously replaces the caps on the tubes of paint, which are spread haphazardly around his palette.

He glances quickly at the wooden clock hanging on the wall, another gift from his friend Brother Haas. It is now seven minutes before seven, and he is due in the chapel. He takes off the purple flannel button down shirt he wears to keep paint off of his "good" clothes and turns off the light. He closes the door leaving behind twenty-five recently completed paintings, all of which will stay in the studio until he has enough time to frame them. He takes the elevator back down to the first floor and heads to the chapel. At 6:55 A.M. he walks through the side entrance of the school's chapel.

At the same time, Melanie Selva is rolling out of bed in the room where she has lived for the last year and a half since she moved into the Girls Hope home in the middle of her freshman year. There is nothing between Melanie and the rest of her day except her slightly furrowed brow and bleary eyes, which a warm shower may be able to eradicate.

Melanie has been living at the Girls Hope home in suburban Evanston for the past year and a half since her grandmother moved into a nursing home in the middle of her freshman year. During her first year at Loyola she studied religion with Maureen Cogan, a veteran of Loyola's theology department. Over the years, Mrs. Cogan has begun her class with a brief prayer. And she has always offered her students the chance to pray for certain intentions.

Historically, her students, freshmen in particular, have not taken advantage of the opportunity to pray in class. That's why she was surprised when Melanie, the diminutive freshman that sat in the front left corner of the room spoke up, "I'd like to pray for my grandmother who is sick."

Mrs. Cogan then coaxed the class into responding, "Lord hear our prayer."

For the next two months, Melanie continued to pray on a daily basis for her grandmother. Her classmates seemed to respect the relationship she must have had with her grandmother, though no one asked her about it. Nobody knew that she had been living with her grandmother, Anna, since January of her fifth grade year when her father and older brother Andrew were killed in a car accident. No one knew that her mother had left and had not been heard from for the last twelve years.

She had moved in with her grandma the day after the rest of her family had been killed. They had always been close, but she had never spent even so much as a night at her grandmother's apartment in Rogers Park, a neighborhood on the north side of the city, near the campus of Loyola University. She transferred from St. Athanasius in Evanston, where her family had lived, to St. Margaret Mary, a grade school not far from her grandma's place. Initially, Melanie and her grandma had little to say to one another. They were both dealing with the loss of family members, Melanie, with her father and brother. Anna on the other hand, was grieving for her only son and grandson.

By year's end however, they had begun to forge a beautiful friendship. Melanie came home from school and her after school sports everyday and worked on her homework until her grandmother began to prepare dinner. Then she would go to the kitchen, and the two of them would cook together, tasting and testing their simple meals often, sometimes eating most of it before they had even sat down at the table.

When they did sit down together they would talk about their respective days. Melanie's stories were usually livelier than those of her grandma, who left the apartment only to run necessary errands and stock up on food. Her grandmother would listen patiently as she recounted her day, what she ate for lunch, what they did in class, who she played with during the recess. They needed each other; they needed the conversation, the company, and the reality. Occasionally they let the conversation meander late into the evening. Melanie's grandmother would begin to tell stories about her childhood, or her visit to Italy in 1974. Her life at present was not terribly exciting, but her stories fascinated Melanie who had only been to St. Louis twice and Florida once. They talked about Melanie's classes, and when the grade cards arrived, her grandmother went over them closely with her, prodding her constantly trying to determine if she was in fact doing her best work.

Just before summer of her sixth grade year, only a year and a half after her father and brother had been killed, Melanie noticed her grandmother set down the knife she was using to chop onions to add to the spaghetti sauce the two of them were preparing in the cramped kitchen. Her grandmother's face tightened in pain as she rubbed the knuckles on her left hand.

"You okay, Gram?"

"Yeah Mel, my hands are hurting me. I don't know what the problem is but they have been swelling up and getting very tender the last couple of days."

When her grandmother visited the doctor a week later he told her that she had developed a surprisingly late case of rheumatoid arthritis. The next few months proved unfortunately that Anna's condition was not an isolated flare-up, but rather a chronic case.

By the time Melanie was in the eighth grade, she had ceased participating in after-school activities. She came home everyday to check on her grandmother, who could not get out of bed without the help of medicine. Her body had been ravaged by the arthritis. It was as if her joints had frozen. She could barely move them, and without her medication, it was incredibly painful to do so.

Melanie had been a godsend. As her grandma's condition slowly worsened, she had simply assumed more of the responsibilities. They had many of their meals delivered by Meals on Wheels, but sometimes Melanie prepared simple dinners for the two of them. They ate at the table Melanie had moved into her grandma's bedroom. In the evenings she would rub lotion into grandmother's gnarled ankles and wrists. Melanie took care of the apartment, taking out the garbage, cleaning the bathrooms, and sweeping the floors.

At the end of her eighth grade year, Melanie applied to Loyola Academy and was accepted. Her freshman year went well. She made the first honor roll in her first quarter. She dedicated herself to her schoolwork. She used the lengthy bus rides to and from Loyola to read and the time after her grandmother had gone to sleep to do the remainder of her homework. Her grandmother was all that she had left, and she was determined to take care of her.

Thus it came as a huge surprise when, in November of her freshman year, her grandmother called her into her bedroom. Anna was sitting up in the bed, resting awkwardly on a stack of pillows. As soon as Melanie came in she patted the edge of the mattress with her contorted fingers. "Mel, come sit down." As soon as Melanie positioned herself on the edge of the bed, facing her grandma, she began to speak. "You're an angel Melanie." As she said this, her grandmother's voice cracked. "You have been so good to me. But you've never been a kid. All this time you haven't had a chance to be a kid." She was right. In Melanie's first three months at Loyola, she hadn't really made any friends. She wasn't involved in any activities, and she hadn't told anyone about her situation at home. She just got on the bus everyday and went home. "You should be doing other things."

"No grandma," Melanie interrupted. "I like being here with you."

"I know you do. And I love having you here. You are the best thing in my life. But you can't take care of me forever. I am getting sicker, and I need to be in a place where I can get more attention. And you need to have a life of your own."

Melanie said nothing, though she wondered how she would be able to have a life without her grandmother, who was her only surviving family member. Then her grandmother told her about the Girls Hope Program. She applied and was accepted.

As Melanie rises, Patrick Martin continues to sleep soundly in the McDermott house, where he has been staying since the beginning of the school year. Tim Ryan reads the paper, his briefcase laid carefully at his feet as his city bound commuter train rolls away from the train station in Winnetka. Father Norm Harland, SJ, has fallen asleep but is awakened by the sound of a nurse entering his room and the smell of thin, slightly overcooked hospital kitchen pancakes.

Every morning one of the Jesuit priests says mass in Loyola's chapel. A few students, some faculty and staff and maybe even a couple neighbors usually attend the mass. This morning, as usual, Brother Small is in the chapel twenty-five minutes early. He goes about preparing the chapel for mass by lighting the candles on the altar and bringing out a chalice, the cup used for consecrating the bread and wine. Then he pours the water and wine and sets them on the altar. He chooses music, usually something slow and meditative, and then plays it on the stereo before mass begins.

He stays behind the scenes until the mass commences, then he makes his way into the chapel and sits amongst the students and teachers.

At 7:20, when mass begins, the hallways are dark and quiet and only an occasional person passes the glass doors at the back of the chapel. The teachers are arriving, and a couple of early bird students are making their way into the school for extra study time or early meetings or a quick breakfast in the cafeteria.

Brother Small does the first reading at today's mass. He reads the following passage deliberately and carefully. He clears his throat, and begins, "A reading from the letter of Paul to the Philippians. 'Be imitators of me, my brothers. Take as your guide those who follow the example that we set.'" He pauses for a moment and looks up at Hernan O. Llerena, a Spanish teacher who left a career as an amateur boxer to come to Loyola nearly thirty years ago. For the last three years, Señor Llerena, as the students affectionately refer to him, has planned to retire. But each fall he has come back to Loyola, unable to leave he says, "until my last group of students is done with their senior year." So he has stopped teaching freshmen, and is instructing only upper-classmen.

"'Unfortunately, many go about in a way which shows them to be enemies of the cross of Christ. I have often said this to you before; this time I say it with tears in my eyes.'" He pauses again. This time he looks to his left. A student is sitting in the back of the chapel. He is still wearing his backpack and he has his head buried in his hands.

"'Such as these will end in disaster! Their only god is their belly and their glory is in their shame. I am talking about those who are set upon the things of this world. As you well know, we have our citizenship in heaven; it is from there that we eagerly await the coming of our savior, the Lord Jesus Christ.'" He pauses again. This time he looks towards the back of the chapel where he sees one of his coworkers, Victor Castillo, sauntering past the doors to the chapel on his way into work. Just before he disappears from sight, Victor glances into the chapel, notices Brother Small and smiles. Victor has been working as a maintenance man and security guard at Loyola for the past ten years. He is now one year away from graduating from Northeastern University with a degree in Criminal Justice. For the past three years he has been taking classes at night and working full time at Loyola during the days.

When Victor came to Loyola ten years ago, he began working as part of the building maintenance staff. In his first few years he worked closely with Brother Small, and he looks back on those years fondly. "He's a great man," Victor says of Brother Small. "He's great to everybody, everybody he meets or works with, and he's willing to help anybody with anything."

"'He will give a new form to this lowly body of ours and remake it according to the pattern of his glorified body, by his power subject to everything to himself. For these reasons, my brothers, you whom I so love and long for, you who are my joy and my crown, continue, my dear ones, to stand firm in the Lord.'" Brother Small pauses once more. This time he looks at the feet of the two people sitting in the front row of the chapel. One of them must be a student, for he is wearing gym shoes. The other has on a pair of perfectly shined black leather wingtips.

"'This is the Word of the Lord.'"

Twenty minutes later the mass is nearly over, and the halls are now bright; there is movement and noise everywhere. Students stream by the glass doors as they make their way into school from the parking lot. On the other side of the glass doors in the relative quiet of the chapel, Brother Small hands the bread of life to those attending mass. He looks at home in the chapel. He stands on the same level as those receiving communion. As each person approaches him, he bends and gently places the bread in their hands. "The body of Christ," he says.

His six foot three frame bends to accommodate everyone, from the shortest freshman to the woman in the wheelchair. His words to each of them are the same: "The body of Christ." As he stands up from the last person, he glances through the glass doors. There, too, is the body of Christ out there in the midst of the students.

Some of them are hurrying; some walk slowly; some glance quickly into the chapel; some stand still talking; some look lost. His message and gift to them is the same: the body of Christ. One of his occasional duties at mass is to share literally the body of Christ, the consecrated bread with those wishing to receive it. As a Jesuit, his responsibilities are very similar. He tries to share the mystical body of Christ with everyone, those willing to receive it as well as those reluctant to accept it or unaware of its existence. I don't mean that he walks around school handing out wafers of unleavened bread. Rather, he tries to help the people around him see Christ. He shares his relationship with Christ with everybody, especially the students at Loyola.

Loyola Academy, in the tradition of college preparatory education, encourages growth not only academically but more importantly, spiritually and personally.

The entire school is located in a single building in Wilmette, a suburb just north of Chicago. The school was originally founded as a preparatory school for Loyola University, and it was located on their lakeshore campus in Chicago. Loyola Academy was founded in 1909 and graduated its first class in 1911.

In 1963 the school moved north to Wilmette. Now it is located just off the Edens Expressway, the main north-south artery running into and out of the city. The school was built on a relatively small plot of land between Lake St. and Happ Rd. It is bordered on the east by the Edens and on the west by Laramie Ave. It sits amongst tree-lined streets in an attractive residential area. There is a gas station and a Dairy Queen across the street, and the second hole of the Wilmette Public Golf Course is just a couple blocks away.

The school presently houses 2,000 students, making it the largest Jesuit school in the United States. Loyola is also home to ten Jesuits. Thirty years ago when Brother Small began at Loyola there were 50 Jesuits and just over 1,000 students. The school has grown rapidly since it moved to the Wilmette campus and much of that growth can be attributed to the decision by the school's board of trustees to open Loyola's doors to women.

In the spring of 1994, Marillac High School, an all girls school run by the Daughters of Charity, closed as its enrollment fell to a point so low that it could no longer survive. The following fall, Loyola and Marillac merged, retaining Loyola's name but fundamentally altering the identity of the school. A school of fifteen hundred boys was transformed into a school of two thousand boys and girls almost overnight.

The change has filled the hallways as the school has grown and grown, and consequently made it difficult to reach each and every student with a little bit of the Jesuit influence that makes Loyola such a special place.

Loyola prides itself on its Jesuit heritage, and education is a central element of Jesuit philosophy and theology. Jesuit education is unique, not only because of its quality, but also because of the spirituality that drives the quality of education. Loyola is a good academic high school; some may say it's a great school. But without the Jesuit influence and theology, it would be nothing more than your average suburban high school.

The introduction of Jesuit values and ideals to the educational setting brings the school to life. It is more than an expensive private school or a good academic school. It is a community working towards assimilating the values of Christianity into its day-to-day existence.

The Jesuit vision of education is driven by two main principles. The first is the belief that God is present in all things. Gerard Manley Hopkins, one of the great Jesuit poets explains this by saying "The world is charged with the grandeur of God." This idea is one of the central tenets of Jesuit spirituality and an important part of the Jesuit philosophy about life and education. If God is present in everything, then God cannot be separated from academic pursuits. Therefore, one's education becomes a religious endeavor or a sacred process.

The second driving principle behind Jesuit education is the idea that education or the learning process is a catalyst for conversion. Conversion? No, not religious conversion. Conversion in this case means a fundamental change in one's point of view. Consider the apathetic student who approaches his studies with a total lack of enthusiasm. "This stuff is totally pointless," he thinks. He doesn't read the paper because he does not care what is going on in the world.

Then in his government class, he learns about the American legislative system, how it works and why it works. Around the same time, he participates in a one day fast to satisfy a requirement for a religion class. He faints in the twentieth hour of the fast. The fast teaches him that people have to live like that. Kids his age go to bed hungry every night. Not everyone has a life as easy and comfortable as he has.

All of a sudden this student becomes concerned with the world around him. He participates in food drives. He writes letters to his congressman and his senator. He realizes how lucky he is to have an easy life, and he promises himself that he will not take that life for granted.

He will do something to make a difference, whether he gathers food or raises awareness about these problems. What has happened to this kid? He has experienced a conversion. He sees the world differently. He understands that the things in the news affect some people, and for that reason they are important. He has realized that he used to see the world only through his eyes, but now he is able to understand the plight of the hungry, and he wants to do something for these people.

This student's change is just one example of a conversion. Conversion as stated does not have to be an explicitly religious experience, just a change in one's understanding or perception that affects the way they see the world and the way that they live from day to day. St. Ignatius believed that individualized guidance and self-reflection were the best ways to foster conversion, or to come to the realization that God is in fact present in all things. This realization will theoretically forever change the way the student understands the world.

The Jesuits at Loyola strive to educate their students according to these driving principles. Their goal is to help students become open to growth, intellectually competent, religious, loving, and committed to justice. Essentially they are committed to educating well-rounded men and women who will serve others. But Loyola's Jesuits' ability to effectively educate all of their students this way is decreasing as the number of students continues to increase and the number of Jesuits continues to decline.

As long as Jesuit education relies in some sense on the idea of conversion, it relies on the idea of individualized guidance. These ideas are at the center of Loyola's teaching philosophy. Even so, many of Loyola's students may never learn them because in their four years here, they never get to know a Jesuit personally or have a Jesuit as a teacher. Today the students at Loyola outnumber the Jesuits by a ratio of two hundred to one, and the students outnumber the teaching Jesuits by a ratio of one thousand to one. How can one Jesuit individually guide two hundred students? It's virtually impossible, especially when most of the Jesuits have little if any contact with the students at the school.

Many of Loyola's teachers can do this, but as lay people with families they just don't have as much time. I don't mean to undermine their efforts; there are a number of truly amazing lay people at Loyola who have committed their lives to educating Loyola's students according to Jesuit ideals. But as long as the Jesuit population continues to shrink and the student body continues to grow, this process of education through conversion will become more and more difficult.

It's no one's fault that the Jesuits cannot reach all of the students, although it is unfortunate. The number of Jesuits in this country is decreasing rapidly. Fewer and fewer men are entering the Jesuits each year. Right now Loyola has only two full time teaching Jesuits compared to thirty years ago when well over half of the teachers there were Jesuits. Most of the rest of Loyola's Jesuits work as administrators. The school has a Jesuit headmaster, a Jesuit president, a Jesuit alumni director, and also a Jesuit carpenter.

Throughout his normal day, Brother Small does not have an opportunity to meet a lot of students. His workshop is located in the basement of the school, just down the hall from the ministry department and across from the cafeteria. Even though he is in an area with a lot of student traffic and he has an open door policy, not many students ever make it into Brother Small's shop. Since he does not get to teach, he doesn't get to meet as many students as he would like. Because of this, not too many students know him well enough to feel comfortable popping their heads into his shop.

Despite all this, Brother Small has tried to meet as many students as possible. He believes so deeply in the ideals of Jesuit life and Jesuit education that he makes a tremendous effort to share them with the students. His responsibilities at the school do not require him to work with, or for that matter have any contact at all with the students. Yet, he always leaves his door open. Adults, children, teachers and students are all welcome in his workshop. He can't ever meet every student at Loyola, and it is probably impossible to see to it that every student will have some kind of meaningful encounter with the Jesuits at Loyola or experience a conversion, but this has not stopped him from trying. He doesn't dwell on the negatives, he simply sets out to create more positives.

Brother Small tries to help these students search for spirituality, find God, and live with God. "This is a very simple thing," he explains, "but whenever I walk the halls, I try to greet every student I see just to let them know that I am interested in them and in their lives. I also hope that my presence in the hallways or in the school might eventually have some bearing on their outlook on life. Maybe when they see me in the halls, they think, 'Okay, here is a guy who doesn't own anything, and doesn't have much going for him. But still he is happy, so there must be something to his life.' So when they are talking amongst themselves or looking into it on their own, they'll start to see a difference between people who are angry with the world and people who are happy with the world. And then maybe they will begin to try to live like those people who are happy with the world."

Setting an example for people is one thing; actively helping or serving them is an entirely different thing. "Is bringing people to God or helping them see God and come to know God part of your work?"

"Yes, the whole idea of St. Ignatius is this, in a nutshell, in a sentence: I want to save my soul, and I want to help others to do the same. Now, I'll be honest; I don't think about that every hour of the day or every time I do something, but I have tried to make it a way of life. Without concentrating on it all the time and in every situation, you can do it if you live your life properly and you love people. You'll know what to do for them. Also, people watch your actions, sometimes consciously and sometimes subconsciously. And they can tell if you are a good person or a bad person, and if you are a good person you can sway them to try to live a good life too, because you are happy and at peace, and you are living a good life."

"Do you love the people you work with, the people you serve?"

"The longer I am at Loyola, the more I love the students, the little boys and girls, and the young men and women, and the more I want to do for them. And I'm sure that's not me, but Christ working through me. If people ever see me, I want them not to see me, but to see Christ working through me."

Brother Small once said, "If I had the ability I'd love to teach. That way I'd have a chance to meet and know so many more students." His desire to help people, to facilitate conversion, to bring people to God, is so great, that his mind is constantly coming up with new ways to do it.

As he ponders the impossibility of teaching, it's almost as if Brother Small forgets his art lessons. He does teach. Every Sunday he takes time out of his weekend schedule to give art lessons to anyone who wants them. He has worked with students as young as five years old as well as some as old as eighteen. He has tutored some very talented artists, as well as some who appeared to have just discovered the pencil. Brother Small will invite the kids to school on the weekends and open up either the library or one of the school's art studios.

These classes are not for credit; there is no grade. Kids come to Brother Small because they want to learn how to draw or paint, not because they need the class to graduate, or because it will be an easy A. They learn from him, and they have fun. Brother Small gives every student a three ring binder, and he instructs them to keep individual work in that binder. They begin by drawing. Some will complete a number of paintings by the time they are done with his classes; some will never get beyond basic drawing.

This Sunday Brother Small expects only three students for the weekly lessons. These three are all working on paintings, so they will be down in his workshop rather than in the library. These three students, Leigh and Isabelle Dunham and Ralph Masterson, have been taking lessons for about a year and a half.

In the first year, Brother Small taught them drawing. He would bring an object to class and then sit with the three of them as they drew. He tried to help them to see the object of the drawing in a clearer way. "What is the shape?" he would ask them constantly. "Where are the edges? Are they hard or soft? Where is the light, and where are the shadows it creates?" If they could see the subject and understand it, then they could do a better of job of recreating it on a piece of paper. He encouraged them. No matter how good or bad a drawing might have been, Brother Small always leaned over the artist's shoulder and said, "Oh this is wonderful. It's absolutely beautiful." Then he took the pencil and showed them how to make a few changes to make it even better. He never criticized, and he never used negative language. These three, Leigh, Isabelle and Ralph, all did very well on their drawings. So after a few months Brother Small asked them if they would like to try painting.

The three of them, whose talents varied considerably, responded enthusiastically. Since then Leigh, a seventh grader and the most talented of the three artists, has finished two paintings. One is an Edward Hopper landscape scene, and more recently, she did a copy of Mary Cassatt's "Girl with a Large Straw Hat." Her little sister, Isabelle, is only five, and she is still working on her first painting, which is of Santa Claus.

Ralph has recently finished his first painting, also an Edward Hopper. Last Sunday the three of them came over to Loyola. Isabelle continued to work on her Santa Claus painting, while Brother Small helped Ralph frame his recently completed copy of "Rooms by the Sea."

Leigh paged through some of Brother Small's art books as she waited patiently to work on framing her Mary Cassatt. On the other side of the room, Brother Small was explaining to Ralph that the frame they were building was made out of real gold.

"This stuff here is real gold, Ralph."

"No, it's not. I'm not stupid," Ralph replied indignantly, brushing his blonde hair out of his bright blue eyes.

"Oh, this is good stuff," he told Ralph. "It's probably worth a hundred dollars. Right, Leigh?"

"Right," she replied with a wide smile.

"If this was real gold, it would be worth a lot more than a hundred dollars," Ralph sneered as if insisting that Brother Small had no idea what he was talking about. He seemed to forget that Brother Small had spent months guiding him through this painting and was now framing it for free. The frame was not gold; they both knew that, but Ralph's bitter denial of the fact suggested that he might have valued the idea of gold more than he valued the chance to work with Brother Small. But Brother Small continued to help him through the framing process, letting Ralph do much of the work himself. Brother Small never uttered an unkind word; he just explained how to frame the picture, step by easy step, and physically guided him through the more difficult steps.

When Ralph left fifteen minutes later with his framed picture under his arm, he neglected to say thanks, although he did say, "I'll see you next weekend." Brother Small closed the door behind him and walked back towards the girls saying to himself, "What a nice boy."

Ralph was not a nice boy; he did not even seem like an okay kid; he seemed to me to be a spoiled brat. He was loud and ungrateful. But Brother Small saw something else in him. I don't know what, because I didn't see it. Behind the loud obnoxious kid, he must have seen another person, a nice person who just did not know how to be nice. Brother Small was trying to show him how to do this, not through words or actions, but through a persistent and obvious gift of kindness. No matter what this kid did or said, Brother Small welcomed him into his shop and treated him with kindness and care. He treats everyone like this.

After Ralph left, he walked across the room to the easel where Isabelle was dipping her paintbrush into a glob of red paint and spreading it around the Santa Claus. "Oh, Isabelle, this is just great," he said bending down and looking over her shoulder. "Leigh, come over here and look at how good your sister's painting is." Then he pointed to a spot where the red paint covered a big part of Santa's white beard. "Now, when you get your white paint out, let's just go along here, and even out the shape of the beard. Okay, honey?"

"Okay," she said as she twisted her head around to look at him, her eyes wide with excitement for being the object of his attention and praise. When their eyes connected, she grinned broadly and then swung her head back towards the painting. He told her again that it was a beautiful painting. She giggled and then dipped her paintbrush back into the red paint and continued her work.

Brother Small walked over to Leigh who sat on one of the wooden stools next to his table saw. Like her little sister, Leigh had her sleeves pushed up, so as to keep them out of the paint. "Any news about the acting?" he asked her.

"I got called back," she said with an embarrassed smile, averting her eyes from Brother Small, "but I didn't get the lead. They gave it to an eighth grader, but in the middle of the play she has a dream for about ten minutes, and I get to be the girl in the dream."

"Oh, well, that's probably the best part in the play anyhow," he told her.

Leigh offered some stories and reflections about the time she has spent with Brother Small. "He's just so nice to everyone," she said. "He's outgoing, and he teaches me so much. He's like a second grandfather to me. He tries to make other people happy; I think that's what makes him so happy. I've been in plays and all, and whatever part I get he always says 'Oh, you were the best one out there.'"

Brother Small has been to see Leigh who was a dancer in "Anything Goes," a featured dancer in "Hello Dolly," and a speaking maid in "Annie." At each play he sat with Leigh's parents and brought a bouquet of flowers to her. "No matter how big or small my part is, he always thinks it's wonderful."

Here's the best part. Brother Small met Leigh's family through a friend. Originally he started teaching Leigh's older sisters, Ashley and Sarah, both are accomplished artists, and then he invited the younger girls. These are not his nieces, goddaughters, or close family friends. They are friends of a friend of his. Yet, he treats these girls like they are part of his family, never missing a play and always bringing flowers. It's as if everyone he meets is in fact part of his family

Once they had finished their painting and artwork, Brother Small took the two girls home, but they didn't go straight home. He stopped at Homer's Ice Cream shop where he bought them both an ice cream cone. Then he dropped them off at their house in Wilmette and headed back to Loyola to do some of his own artwork.

The art lessons are a good example of some of the small things in Brother Small's life that have grown to become very big meaningful things. The art classes have obviously grown in size over time, but that is not really the important thing. The real lessons learned in his art classes are not only about art but also about life. Mary McCall, one of Brother Small's early art students, said, "Taking Brother Small's art lessons has definitely taught me about art, but I came away from the experience with so much more than artistic skills. Each one of us was so fortunate just to be able to observe a person like Brother Small in a closed environment. I look back now and I realize that my interaction with him has meant so much more to me than I've ever known."

Brother Small's choice to spend an hour or two each weekend giving free art lessons may seem insignificant in the big picture. So far none of the artists under his tutelage have gone on to artistic careers. But, that doesn't matter at all to Brother Small; that is not why he teaches the classes. He does it because he enjoys it, and because he thinks the kids enjoy it.

And because they enjoy it, many of them do learn a lot, and they become very accomplished amateur artists. But more importantly, some of the kids learn something much greater than drawing or painting from Brother Small. They see him doing this for free. In that alone they see something different. How often do people, other than parents take time out of their schedules to sit down and work on an individual basis with kids? Maybe they wonder why he is doing this, but then they see that there is a reward. He loves what he is doing, and it makes him happy. He likes showing them how to draw; for him this is great fun. Indirectly he shows these kids that some of the best things in life truly can be free. Mary McCall noted, "Brother Small taught me the insignificance of material possessions. As little girls we didn't understand or accept the concept that he didn't own anything. I remember him explaining that he gave up his possessions when he decided to devote his life to the Lord, that there was nothing he needed that the Lord could not or would not provide him. What an amazing thing to reinforce to kids at such an insecure age."

He also had a special influence on the life of Margaret Kearney, one of his first female art students, who reflected on her relationship with Brother Small, "He has played a role in the development of my spirituality. He has been one of the biggest role models in my life. It is hard not to try to mimic some of the aspects of his life . . . He has never forced his beliefs on me, which says to me that he has that much more of an understanding of the meaning of religion and spirituality."

Mary McCall claims, too, "Brother Small had a profound impact on my spirituality, and my person as a whole . . . As far as spirituality is concerned, Brother Small's example spoke more to me than any religious education I had received at that point in my life."

Some of his students don't see these greater lessons right away, and some of them never do. Like Margaret said, Brother Small does not force his ideas or beliefs on people. He is a quiet leader who sets examples and invites others to follow simply by offering encouragement and support. His lessons are usually silent, yet their echoes can be heard loud and clear for years to come. He shows these young people how to live gently and beautifully, how to draw, and how to give freely of themselves to others.

3

To give and not to count the cost

You must give some time to
your fellow men. Even if it's a
little thing, do something for
others-something for which
you get no pay but the
privilege of doing it.

-Albert Schweitzer

Once the morning mass is over, Brother Small straightens up the chapel. It is now nearly eight o' clock, time for breakfast, and the man is getting hungry. He shuts off the lights over the altar and heads towards the Jesuit residence where he will have his usual brief breakfast. He leaves the chapel through the front door and makes his way through the bustling foyer past the centerpiece of the school, the statue of St. Ignatius.

The statue serves as a symbol and a reminder of the values and spirituality espoused by Ignatius, the diminutive Spaniard who founded the Jesuits. Although Brother Small insists that his life is in no way saintly, it bears remarkable similarities to St. Ignatius' life. The two have quite a lot in common; not the least of which is their delight in the exercise of arms.

St. Ignatius was born in 1491, in Azpeitia, a small town in the Basque region of northern Spain. His family was large; he was the youngest of thirteen children. As he grew older, Ignatius developed into a legendary philanderer and gambler. He was by all accounts a vain young man. He did, however, grow to be a deadly swordsman and a great enthusiast of weaponry, as he states in the opening lines of his autobiography.

> Until the age of twenty-six he was a man given over to
> the vanities of the world; with a great and vain desire to win

fame he delighted especially in the exercise of arms. (St. Ignatius, 21)

James Small was born on January 10, 1922, more than 400 years after the birth of St. Ignatius. He, too, came from a large family; he was the second of six children. Jim grew up in a family of policemen. His dad and grandpa both served on the police force and their work fascinated him. As a youngster, Jim spent many mornings watching his dad dress for work. He loved the creased blue uniforms, the shoes and, especially, the gun.

In fact, when he was just four and a half years old, Jim managed to find his dad's 38 Colt handgun. He was a busy child, busy causing trouble or busy looking for it. Jim was no holy roller; he was a normal hell-raising kid. He had never seen a gun fired anywhere other than in some of the western movies he saw on Saturday afternoons. When he was in the first grade, his father had explained what a gun was, how it worked, and what policemen used their guns for. Along with that explanation came a very strict warning to never ever go near the guns.

That was all the encouragement Jim needed to try one of the guns out for himself. He became consumed with the idea of holding and possibly firing the gun. He bided his time until he knew he would be able to get into his parent's bedroom, where the gun was stored. One afternoon, minutes after he'd gotten home from school, Jim got his chance when the doorbell rang. He followed his mom to the door.

"Hi, Margaret, come on in," Jim's mom said. It was Mrs. Gallagher, Jim's best friend's mom. As soon as she was in the house, Jim realized his opportunity. He turned and headed for his parents' bedroom, hardly hearing the two women talking about the weather or dresses or whatever else they always talked about.

Once he made it into the bedroom, he rifled through his dad's belongings in the closet until he found the gun. He backed slowly out of the closet and made his way over to the bed. He stood on his tiptoes, and hopped gently up onto the high bed, all the time never taking his hands off the gun.

He sat there quietly, gazing intently at the shining metal of the magnificent pistol. He turned it over in his hands, inspecting each part. He looked down the barrel, rubbed the handle and carefully touched the trigger. He was going to put the gun back into the closet, but then he decided since he had it out, he should at least shoot it once. He thought that if he fired it into the wall, no one would ever know he had even used it, unless they happened to find the small hole he expected it would leave.

He knelt on the bed, with his knees spread far apart. He pointed the gun at the wall behind the bed, which did not have any windows. It was the wall between his parents' room and the living room, where his mom and Mrs. Gallagher were now sitting. He closed one eye and reached his little finger around to the trigger. Just before he pulled it, he had a better idea. Rather than shoot into the wall, he would shoot into a pillow. The pillow, he thought, would silence the gun and might even stop the travel of the bullet. He figured if he took off the pillowcase, he could shoot into the pillow and then put the pillowcase back on the pillow and no one would ever know about it. So he crawled to the head of the bed where he removed the pillowcase from one of the pillows.

He put the pillow down right in front of his knees. He pushed the barrel of the gun into the pillow and fired. The bullet traveled through the pillow, the mattress, and the box spring, until it finally lodged in the wooden floor of his parent's bedroom. Jim was knocked off his knees when he fired the gun and laid flat on his back on the mattress thinking that the gun was a little bit more powerful than he had expected. His mother was in the bedroom almost instantly, her face contorted by fear and then anger. She stood glaring at him while he sat on her bed with feathers from the pillow and smoke from the gun floating around his head.

Jim's one pre-adolescent shooting incident was just the beginning of his attraction to weaponry. Like Ignatius, Jim's fascination with guns intensified, as he grew older and became a man of the world.

When he left the Jesuit seminary in Milford, Ohio at the age of nineteen, he moved back in with his parents and got a job working as one of about fifteen hundred machinists at Goodman Manufacturing, a Chicago based company that produced mining equipment that is still in use today in mines all over the country

Jim had been working at Goodman for well over a year when World War II erupted. On Dec. 7, 1941, the Japanese attacked Pearl Harbor. A day later, the United States declared war.

From the beginning, Jim Small wanted to fight in this war. He wanted to defend his country so much that he felt himself drawn to the war. So, he tried to sign up, but the Navy would not accept him. As soon as the American armed forces began to mobilize, the government had contracted Goodman Manufacturing to mass-produce shells and artillery. Because Jim was working for a company contributing to the war effort, the navy refused to accept his services. They insisted his work there was just as important as anything he could do on the sea or overseas. So through the first six months of the war, Jim Small stayed at home and worked dutifully at Goodman.

Every once in a while, he would be at the market or at church and he would see the parents of one of his friends.

"Jim, how are you?"

"Fine, and you, Mrs. Gallagher?"

"We're doing well; we just got a letter from Joe. His ship is returning to Pearl Harbor for a week, and then they will head back to the Islands."

"Is he doing okay?"

"As well as can be expected I guess," their ashen faces told a different story, a sober story of a life of constant worry and fear. "How are you?"

"Oh, just fine, I'm still working down at Goodman, managing to keep busy."

"Well, you're lucky to be here; your parents are lucky to have you here."

"I know."

"Well, Jimmy, will you please say a prayer for Joe, just so that he gets home safely, because me and his father are worried something terrible about him."

"I will. I will."

Jim knew he was lucky to be home, but still he was not too happy about it. He felt it was his duty to serve the country in which he lived. He wanted to be there, but they wouldn't let him. He felt guilty about being home. His friends were there, fighting; some had died.

He was home living the good life. His friend's parents must have resented him. Some of his friends might have even resented his position. It was understandable. Every night he went to sleep in his own bed under a safe sky. Finally, he quit his job at Goodman so that he could join the Navy and go overseas.

After three grinding months of boot camp, and three weeks of horribly mundane basic training, Jim was sent to the West Coast where he was to await his first real assignment. A personnel attack ship was set to leave San Francisco with just over five hundred sailors, all of whom were being transferred to Pearl Harbor. In addition to the regular sailors, a hundred supernumeraries also made the journey to Pearl Harbor. Supernumeraries traveled on the ship as substitutes. They were there to fill in if any of the regular or experienced sailors fell ill or were injured during the voyage. Jim Small was the last supernumerary, literally the last man on the ship.

The voyage to Pearl Harbor was a nightmare. In all his life Jim had never been on a boat for more than an hour at a time, let alone a week on the Pacific Ocean. The seas were rough for their one-week journey and Jim was violently ill from the moment he passed under the Golden Gate Bridge until he arrived in Pearl Harbor. In fact, the seas were so rough that the veteran sailors, the ship's crew and the gun crew were all suffering from seasickness, not just the newly enlisted men.

During his second night on ship, the siren was sounded, warning the sailors that a Japanese submarine had been sighted in the vicinity of the ship. Jim had given up at this point; he was so sick that he says,

"I wished the torpedo would hit the ship and sink us. I was so sick I wasn't thinking clearly." But the torpedo did not hit the ship, and during the alert all of the sailors had to come up to the deck.

Jim reluctantly rolled out of his bunk and walked queasily to the ladder out of the bunkroom. The ladder was covered in vomit. Jim began the climb up gripping the ladder tightly. The ship continued to rock back and forth and, each time it rocked, some more vomit from the floor above cascaded down the ladder and washed over his hands. When the alert ended, Jim climbed all the way back down to his bunk, feeling worse than he had before. He climbed into bed, and did not get back out until the ship arrived at Pearl Harbor four and a half days later. In that time he ate only eight pieces of Christmas candy.

He stayed at Pearl Harbor for the remainder of the war. He worked in the submarine base fire department, which was very similar to any city's fire department. He started out as a nozzle man, or a standard firefighter. By the end of the war he was the second chief of the fire department at the submarine base. He spent twenty-seven months as a fire fighter at Pearl Harbor.

"Why did you want to fight in the war so badly? Would you do it over again?"

"When you're young, you're not really afraid of things, so you take chances, and you want to be a hero and all. I felt like I should go because it was the right thing to do. I had a responsibility. And to be quite honest, at that age I also wanted to go because I thought it might be exciting.

I feel a lot different about war now than I did then. I don't think there is such a thing as a just war. I used to believe in war, obviously; I fought in one. But I used to think our military was great and I got excited about good battles, especially the ones we won. Our military says that it is their profession to protect us. It is, but it is also for them to kill other people. It's scary and it's sad. I can't get excited about it anymore. The loss of life saddens me, no matter whose life it is. Does it really matter whose life it is?

When I was in the service, I used to think it was great for our pilots to keep track of how many planes they had shot down by painting those little German and Japanese flags on the sides of their planes. The more kills you had, the better you were. But, I never really thought about it. It doesn't take much thought either. When I thought of those soldiers as people, rather than little flags, I felt very differently about it.

How would our pilots like to go meet the families of those boys they shot down? They were probably the same age; maybe they had the same kind of education, maybe they were from the same size family. How would they like to meet them? Can you imagine meeting them? How would that feel? How would they like to look that boy's mother in the eyes, and say, 'I shot down your son. I killed your son, and I painted this flag on the side of my plane to show I killed him.' You've got to look deeper. I am just beginning to realize how crazy all of that stuff is. War is so asinine. We want peace so we are going to kill all these people to make peace. It doesn't make sense at all."

Once the war ended Jim traveled home via the Panama Canal and soon thereafter he was discharged from Great Lakes Naval Base. He didn't take any time off; he went back to work immediately for Goodman Manufacturing. After about a year of work, he decided to take the police academy exam, and he passed.

On May 30, 1521, Ignatius' leg was shattered when he was hit with a cannonball. During his recuperation period, he experienced a conversion. He was drawn towards Christ. He could feel the Holy Spirit working in his life, and he felt calm and peaceful at these times. But, he also still yearned for fame, glory, and women. He struggled as he was drawn to both of these very different desires. Eventually he let his old ways die. He stopped chasing women and changed the focus of his life from the quest for fame to the quest for peace. Soon he was well enough to walk again, and he decided it was time for him to go on a journey.

He left Azpeitia for the Holy Land. But he never made it. He was sidetracked at Montserrat, a mountaintop monastery in Spain. While there, he gave away his clothes and sword. He left Montserrat, owning nothing and landed in Manresa, where he lived in a cave and experienced an intense spiritual enlightenment that forever changed the way he saw the world. He ended up in Rome where he began his life of service, which lives on today in the Society of Jesus.

The night before Jim's first day on the job as a policeman his father offered some advice: "Son, if you're going to be working traffic duty down there, you are going to have to know your way around. People are going to be asking you all kinds of questions like 'Where's Goldblatts?' 'Where's Sears?' You are going to have to know where all the important offices are and where all the famous people live." His dad was excited that his son had finally decided to join the force, and it showed. He spoke quickly and enthusiastically. He seemed to truly relish the opportunity to give his son advice on a job he so enjoyed.

That night his dad gave him two maps, two street guides and a directory of addresses, urged him to memorize them and convinced him to take them to work the next day. He did. He tucked them into the deep pockets of his police issue overcoat.

His first day as a police officer was a cold one, extremely cold. It was the end of December and the temperatures had fallen below zero. The wind was howling through the city making everyone colder still. Jim and his new partner Leo Karpinski were working traffic duty at the intersection of State and Monroe, right in the heart of the Loop. Around eleven o'clock, a few hours into his first shift, a man dressed in a black trench coat and a tattered pair of trousers walked up to Jim. He blew into his dirty, callused hands to warm them up and then looked at the two policemen.

Jim looked inquiringly at the man as if to say "Can I help you with anything?" Then the guy yelled into his face, "Yeah, Mo, where's Goldblatts?" His dad had been right; people wanted to know where Goldblatts was. He was taken aback by the way this man treated him; he did, however, direct him to Goldblatts. "Mo." The word rang through his head. "Mo?" Why had the man called him "Mo?" He had expected people to treat him with respect because he was a policeman. They didn't.

"That guy obviously did not respect you because you were a policeman, so what do you think people have to do to earn respect?"

"If you obey the Commandments, that takes care of everything, then you are living a life that is very much worthy of respect. You've also got to look out for little details in your life. Not always the big things, but the little details you can help people with; there are so many small things like that. Even though they are small things, if you keep doing them over and over, people will, little by little, begin to respect you, and they'll know you are a good person.

I think a lot of times we make the mistake of giving people respect for the wrong reasons. I think it's ingrained into human nature. I know I am guilty of it. In the bible you read about it. St. James said a rich man comes in to the temple and you bow to him and tell him to take the first place and some poor fellow comes in and you tell him to take the last place. And we do the same thing: if you see a bum out on West Madison St. you're not going to treat him the same way you treat the president of the bank across the street, although you should. They've both got souls; God would die on the cross for either one of them, but we don't see it that way, and that's not right. I can see that in myself too, I treat wealthy people differently than I treat some poor guy who is working for us and doesn't have anything. It's too bad that I do that, but sometimes I just can't help it. You know, the wealthy people are the ones who buy my paintings; some poor guy is never going to be able to buy one of my paintings."

All in all, his first day on the police force did not go too well. An hour or so after his encounter with the man looking for Goldblatts, Jim faced another question. "Excuse me, sir," a small shivering woman said, "could you direct me to the Palmer House?" As soon as she stopped speaking she buried her face behind the collar of her jacket.

"The Palmer House, sure," replied Jim as he pulled out one of his two guides to the city. He flipped clumsily through the guide with his gloved fingers "Well, it's not in this guide," he said as he handed it to the woman. "If you could just hold this, I'll try another one." The second guide had it, but now he needed to find the map and locate it. "Now if you'll hold this one, I'll just get out my map, and we'll find it here for you." The woman took hold of the second guide with a puzzled look on her face. Jim rooted through the pockets of his overcoat until he found the Chicago street map. He began to unfold it. While fidgeting with the map, he looked up and noticed a sign for the Palmer House directly across the street. "Well, I'll be, there it is there!" he enthusiastically told the lady as he pointed across the street. The woman gave a quick sigh and an even quicker, "Thank you" as she hurried away, leaving Jim fumbling with his collection of street guides and maps.

Despite the frustration of his first day on the job, Jim came to love police work, especially once he was transferred to the Accident Investigation Unit of the Fifth District, which was then located at Forty-eighth and Wabash.

As part of this unit, Jim investigated some of the car accidents that occurred around the city each day, and then assigned blame to one of the two parties. By determining who was at fault in the accidents, the police saved the insurance companies the hassle of investigating the accidents and possibly going to court to determine blame.

The Fifth District was the busiest district in Chicago at that time, and one of the busiest in the country. On any given night, there could be a shooting, a robbery, a rape, a stick-up, or maybe even all four. Despite the fact that Jim worked for the accident investigation department, he found himself doing a great deal of regular police work.

On many occasions, he and his partner would be out investigating an accident and there would be a call about a robbery in progress only blocks away from their investigation. Many times they were the first officers on the scene.

Jim and Joe Bernet, his partner, were wrapping up the paperwork of an accident investigation near 43rd and Michigan when a call came over the radio. "There is a disturbance at 4197 South State St. Officers requested on the scene."

Jim set down his clipboard and started driving; they were just two blocks from this "disturbance." Theirs was the first car on the scene. The specified address was a closed down storefront, but they could hear loud music, glass breaking and people screaming and yelling inside.

Little did the two of them know that, inside the building, the wedding reception of a fifteen-year-old Gypsy girl and a sixty-two-year-old African American man had run amok. They glanced at each other, pulled their guns and made their way slowly to the front door, which was unlocked and opened easily.

Joe swung the door open, but it was pushed closed by a flying chair. "Whoa," he said. This time he slammed the door open and walked in with his gun pointed at the people. No one seemed to notice him. In the corner, one man held another man against the wall trying to strangle him. Another chair flew across the room and hit a man in the back of the head. This man, dressed in a red gown with sequins, ran at the man he thought had thrown the chair and tackled him over a table. It was like a scene from a movie, except that it was probably too weird to have actually been in a movie at that time in America's cinematic history.

"Police! Police!" Jim and Joe yelled. "Everyone calm down." They all disregarded this warning, and the two Police Officers found themselves dodging flying bottles and chairs. They couldn't understand the feverish screams of most of the people in the room.

"What's going on in here?" Joe asked.

"I don't have any idea," Jim replied, ducking out of the way of a flying bottle. They began to make their way through the room breaking up the fights and calming everyone down. After two or three minutes of escalating pandemonium, four more officers arrived on the scene. Just as things began to calm down, there was an explosion in the room. Jim and Joe both ducked and neither of them was hit.

When Jim got off duty early the next morning, he went straight home. As he undressed he noticed something wet in the back of the pants. There was a huge bloodstain just below the waistline of the police issue trousers. So he felt his behind, and sure enough, he was bleeding. He figured he just got nicked by some of the debris from the explosion, so he showered, washed off his wound, and went to bed. In two weeks the cut had healed completely.

"Were you at peace with your life during the war years and your time in the Police Department?"

"At the time I would have definitely said YES. I thought I had peace in my life, or I guess I just assumed that I had peace in my life. But my life then was totally filled with action and movement. I worked a lot and, when I didn't work, I went out to the parties, the dances and the taverns with the fellas, and sometimes with my sister Marge too. I never had enough time to really sit back and think about my life. In reality, I never really thought about being peaceful. But, looking back, I can see that my life was not peaceful at all."

Peaceful or not, Jim did enjoy police work. Chasing criminals and pulling the guns excited him; he thrived on the thrill of pursuit and the 'action' of his profession. He worked on the police department for five years and loved every minute of it. But, it did not last forever. In fact, the turning point that eventually led him away from the police force began as nothing more than a routine accident investigation.

That particular night Jim stood in a brightly lit hallway in Provident Hospital. He and Joe were there following up an investigation of an accident that had happened earlier in the evening. It was a terrible accident; four of the five victims involved were in serious condition.

Jim was talking to the one victim who was well enough to answer his questions. The two of them stood in the hallway opposite each other. Jim had his notebook out and he was quizzing the woman about the details of the accident. Despite the severity of the injuries, it was a routine collision and Jim and his partner were about ready to close their investigation and leave the hospital; it was already 3:00 a.m. on Sunday morning.

Just as he finished up his interview with the woman, a hospital orderly rolled a stretcher down into the hallway and left it right in front of Jim. A man in a tattered tan suit lay on the stretcher. He was dead. He had been shot. There was a bullet wound in his stomach, and blood was still leaking out of his body and staining the clothes around the hole. It was an awful scene but not a totally unfamiliar one.

He had been around dead bodies before. It was never easy, but it was possible to block them out, to view the bodies as evidence or simply as physical machines that no longer functioned properly. It was hard when the body had been the father of two little girls or the only son of an older couple. Having been around death enough, though, Jim usually managed to focus on the work at hand and ignore the life behind the dead body.

But tonight he couldn't. It wasn't this man's family that struck Jim; this guy wasn't even a victim. He had been shot while holding up a store, but he had fired first. He had wounded a police officer. He had committed a crime, a very serious crime. And now he was lying in front of Jim, dead on a stretcher, alone in the hallway of a hospital on the south side of Chicago.

Jim's eyes started to move up and down the man. His hair was wet. Had it been raining? Was he sweating? He had been working. His work is different than most people's but that was how he worked: illegally. What did he need the money for? Did he have kids? His eyes were open and rolled back in his head. The same eyes had stared down the clerk in the store and threatened him, "Give me the money, give it to me now, or I'll kill you. I'll kill you right here."

His clothes were nice; they were worn out, but they were good clothes. They looked like church clothes. But then there was the wound, and the church was gone. Now there was a hole. Where did it go? How deep did the bullet get? There was the blood, some of it dried, most of it still moist. His right hand hung lifelessly off the side of the stretcher. A few hours ago that hand had clutched a revolver. That same hand had thrust the revolver in the face of an innocent man, that hand had almost killed him. That hand had tried to kill a police officer. His body spun; he saw the officer and, with that now lifeless finger, he fired a shot. He had tried to kill, and now he was here dead.

His legs looked normal like any other legs, and on his feet he had a beautiful pair of tan shoes. No one made shoes like those any more. They were genuine leather, but shiny like patent leather. The shoes caught Jim's attention for some reason. The man looked like any other criminal but he had these beautiful shoes on. They were worn in, but they still looked so nice. Jim ran his finger along the bottom of the shoe where the leather met the sole as he thought to himself that this man had worn these shoes many times. They must have taken him so many different places.

Sometime earlier in the day, that man had put those shoes on. He had pulled them onto his feet, wiggled his toes and then tied them up tight. "When he put them on this morning," Jim thought to himself, "he had no idea that he would not be taking them off tonight."

Emotions and thoughts began to pour into his mind. This street thug and his brown shoes challenged Jim to reevaluate his life and his priorities. In the hallway that night, Jim experienced a conversion that would fundamentally change the way he understood his life and his place in the world.

His body was there, but where was he? Jim wondered. Where was the criminal? Where had the man who had committed the crime gone? Where was the man who had been a son, or a brother, or maybe a father? Where was his soul? What would happen to his soul? He had died committing a serious crime. He had died in sin.

Jim's thoughts turned to himself. Life could end too quickly. He knew there would be a day when he too would die, but when would that day come? Until he saw those tan shoes, he did not realize that the day could come tomorrow or it could come fifty years later. But, the possibility of that day coming tomorrow frightened him.

He was thirty years old and all of his friends were married and starting families, but he was still single. "Is this what life is all about?" he started to ask himself. "Is it about going around to the dances with the girls and having a few beers at the taverns with the fellas?" He decided then that he wanted more from life than to just have a good time. He wasn't sure what, but he realized it wasn't worth it to take chances when one's life could end so abruptly.

In the months following his experience in the hospital, Jim spent a good deal of time analyzing his life, asking himself what it was all about. He felt he was being called, but he didn't go immediately. Maybe he was too comfortable in his life; maybe he didn't want to leave his work as a policeman.

He still went out with Marge and the fellas but something was missing. He wasn't having as much fun. He had once been the life of the party, the entertainer. He dazzled his friends with impersonations of others and humorous skits, but after the hospital, he was just going through the motions. Everything had changed.

One night on the drive home from a party Jim said, "Margie, I can't get the vocation (a religious life) out of my mind. I don't want to do it, I like what I am doing, but I feel like I am supposed to do it, and I am being pulled towards it."

"Jim," Marge eventually replied, "if you really feel like this is your calling, that this is what you have to do, then do it. If you don't, it would be like letting a miracle slip right out of your hands."

For two months Jim silently wrestled with the new emotions created by his experience in the hospital and with the satisfaction and comfort he had found in police work.

"How did you decide to join the Jesuits?"

"In the end it came down to consolation and desolation, just like Ignatius said. At the time, I did not know what to call it, but looking back it makes perfect sense. Consolation is, simply, how we tell what is right for us, and more importantly, what is right in relation to God. Consolation is a deep sense of satisfaction, satisfaction in the soul. Desolation, on the other hand is the feeling of emptiness or uneasiness you get when the things you are doing, whether or not they are profitable, are not giving you a deep sense of satisfaction, or a feeling of rightness and peace."

Jim felt he was being called to the Jesuits, but it just didn't seem to make sense. It felt right, but why? He had everything. He had a great job, an exciting job that he thoroughly enjoyed. He had many friends. Most weekends he went on dates with girls. He would be married, when he met the right person. His life made sense. Yet all of a sudden it didn't.

"Were you unhappy with your life before you joined the Jesuits? If you were, what did you hope to find by joining?"

"I enjoyed the life I had before I entered, very much so, so I wouldn't say I was unhappy. However, after I saw the body at the hospital, I came to a realization that the point of life is not just to enjoy yourself and go from one amusement to the next. It is more about being a man for other people. I realized what I should be. I should be a person who helps other people.

My life became empty when I was living just for myself. I enjoyed my life, but I wasn't deeply happy. It's funny how that works. We as humans, no matter how smart we are, seem to think that happiness is just around the corner. We seek happiness in objects, in a promotion at work, more money, new homes, new golf clubs. We think these things will bring us infinite happiness. But, they won't; it's just vanity. I began to realize this, and that's when I decided to join the Jesuits. We must love God now, today: not sometime in the future. The only way to find a deep and lasting happiness is to love and serve God. That's what I was looking for in the Jesuits. I hoped to find peace, save my soul and save others."

In the summer of 1952, Jim told his sister Marge he was reentering the Jesuits in three days. His decision came as a shock to his family, even Marge. His younger brother, Jack, was very ill at the time. He suffered from nephritis, a disease of the kidney, and it looked as though he might not live much longer. Marge questioned the timing of her brother's departure.

"Jimmy, how can you leave now? Jack is dying and you are going to leave now? Can't you wait?"

"Margie, I can't wait. I must do this."

"Now?" she pleaded. "Not now!"

"Margie, I made the arrangements a long time ago, and I have to go now; they expect me down there in a few days.

Before he left for the Jesuit novitiate at Milford, Jim got down on his knees and prayed that God would give his brother's life back. He felt that by joining the Jesuits and giving up much of his life, he could save his brother's. He tried to bargain with God. His bargain failed. One week after he had arrived in Milford, his brother died. Jim returned for the wake and funeral, but no sooner than they had buried his little brother, he hastened back to Milford. Five days later, his younger brother, Bud, and his nephew were involved in a car accident at the intersection of 103rd and Vincennes on the south side of Chicago.

Jim's nephew was killed in the accident and his brother was in serious condition at the hospital. When he got the news down at Milford, Jim went immediately to his superior, "Father, my brother and nephew have been in a bad car accident. My nephew was killed and my brother is still in the hospital. I'd like to go back home to be with my brother and my sister Helen whose boy was killed."

"We're aware of what's happened," said Brother Small's brand new superior, "and we are all very sorry, but we don't think you should go home. We are asking you to stay here. You were just home, and we don't think it would be good for you to go back under similar circumstances."

Encouraging him to stay there? Not good for him? How did these priests know Jim Small already? He had only been there for two weeks. He knew what was good for him: going home to support his brother and sister. But he did not argue or make a fuss. Something told him to turn around and walk away, to accept the fact that he could not go home.

Today, if you ask Brother Small what has been the most significant event or accomplishment in his life, he answers quickly, "Joining the Jesuits. PERIOD!"

"Have you found peace in your life since you have joined the Jesuits?"

"I certainly have. Ever since I joined the society, I've found peace. I'm not going to kid you and say it has always been great. There have been hard times, but I have never regretted my decision to stay, not even for a day; it has been the best decision of my life. Because I have found that peace, it is a fundamental deep peace, no matter what goes wrong, no matter what kinds of disagreements or problems there are, you've got that sense of peace and wholeness and rightness. The Lord makes sure you've always got that."

"Is the peace you've found just a result of you being a part of the society, or is it tied to the life you lead as a Jesuit."

"I think it is just the spiritual life itself, regardless of what your profession is. People in the world, as we say, out in the world, have the same opportunities for peace that the religious have, if they choose to live their lives that way. There are many people with religious vocations who don't achieve peace because they are not living the right kind of life. It's the same way with people out in the world. If they don't live a good life, and do what they know is right, eventually they'll find they just don't have peace of soul."

"Brother Small, what if someone came to you, say a successful lawyer, a forty-five year old father of a Loyola student and said, 'Brother Small, I see that you have peace in your life, and I really envy that, because I don't have it at all. Can you tell me how you've found it, or how I can find it?' What would you tell him?"

"I would say, obey the Commandments. It's a simple answer really. But, it's amazing. It seems so much of the world has just moved away from or totally forgotten about the Commandments. But, if you obey the commandments and you live a good life, you will find peace in your life. I'd also say that you should pray, and let the Holy Spirit tell you what exactly to do. The Holy Spirit will tell you how to live your life through words, experiences and feelings. The Holy Spirit will tell you things I cannot even begin to tell you. But you have to ask, or, at the very least, you have to try to listen."

"Why do you think people have, as you say, moved away from or completely forgotten about the Commandments?"

"It seems to me that some people don't think they (the Commandments) apply to life today, that they are too old, that they were designed for a different time or a different place. But, the Commandments are the very same now that they were thousands of years ago when God first gave them to us, and they will never change; they'll always be the same. And while everybody may look at them, or at any rules and regulations differently, deep down in their soul, they know what is right and wrong, and their conscience will tell them that."

Once he's in the Jesuit residence, he pours himself a bowl of generic corn-flake type cereal and pulls a bagel out of the bag sitting on the countertop in the kitchen. He sits down by himself in the dining room and eats quickly so that he can squeeze in a few more minutes of painting before work begins. He eats quietly and looks out the third story window at the freshman football field. The grass is slowly losing its brilliant green color as late autumn frosts encroach on the warm evenings. Most of the leaves have fallen off the trees and lay scattered around the outskirts of the field.

He takes one last bite of cereal and follows it with the last bit of bagel. He rinses out his dishes and puts them in the dishwasher, wipes his hands on a dishtowel and then returns to his second floor art studio.

This past Tuesday, the father of a Loyola graduate and an acquaintance of Brother Small called.

"Brother Small, Timothy Ryan here."

"Hiya, Tim, how are you?"

"Not too bad Brother. Not too bad, and you?"

"Oh very good, thank you. Now, what can I do for you?"

"My wife, Lynne, turns forty-eight at the end of the week, and we've just remodeled our kitchen. See, she used to have a framed poster hanging in there, but now that we've redone the kitchen I thought a painting would look a lot nicer. Thing is, she really liked this poster and I thought it would be nice to have it copied as a painting . . . and I was hoping you could copy it for me."

"What does the picture look like?"

"Well, it's actually a poster of an old painting, a man and a woman on a beach. The woman is sort of leaning up against a rowboat, and the man is sitting next to her in the sand. I think the artist's name is Paul Stevenson or Steffensen."

"And you need it by the end of the week?"

"Actually, I have a two day meeting in New York beginning on Friday and I won't be home til Saturday night, so I was hoping to have it by Thursday night, so that we could celebrate Lynne's birthday a night early."

"If you can bring the picture over here this afternoon, Tim, I'll do my best. I oughta be able to get it done on time."

"Brother, you are a life saver, I'll bring it over right after I get home from work."

"Good enough, we'll see you then."

As soon as Brother Small got the poster on Tuesday evening, he started working on it. On Wednesday he did not get a chance to paint much because he spent the day at Evanston Hospital with Father Norman Harland, one of his fellow Jesuits who is undergoing cancer treatment. It is now Thursday morning. Mr. Ryan had called Wednesday night and inquired about the painting. Brother Small told him that it was coming along, and he thought he would be able to get it done in time. He told Mr. Ryan he would most likely need every minute right up to eight o'clock Thursday evening to finish it though. Brother Small knows it will be close; so far he has done part of the beach, the boat, and the figures. He still needs to finish the beach and add the dunes, as well as the lady's head and face, not to mention the water and the sky. "No problem," he told Mr. Ryan this morning; he's confident he can finish it if he puts in a little extra time.

Today he has just over fifteen minutes to paint before work. He will have to take advantage of every minute if he hopes to have the painting done by eight o'clock this evening.

He flips on his beat up radio, a standard portable stereo—well, at some point in time it was standard, but now it is at least fifteen years old. The antenna is twisted and bent, and the handle has fallen off the top of the radio, which is covered with splotches and sprinkles of every different color of paint. But it still works.

He pulls the dirty purple shirt he wears while painting over the worn white button down shirt he is already wearing. Then he sits down in his chair, a standard swivel chair that he has rebuilt to be as tall as the stool he used to use. He sits for a few moments and studies the copy of the Ryans' poster. He rummages through his tubes of paint, eventually pulling three different colored tubes out of the mix. He unscrews the cap on each tube, white, red, and yellow, and squirts the paint into the few clear spots on his chaotic palette. He wipes his brush to make sure it is still clean. The old radio plays quietly in the corner, a commercial comes to an end, and the man on the radio says, "Now for the drive in to work we will give you the Chicago Symphony Orchestra's rendition of Tchaikovsky's *1812 Overture*." With that Brother Small begins to paint.

He dips his brush into the white paint, moving some of it to a clean spot on the fringe of his palette. He goes back for a speck of red paint, and then a bit of yellow. He mixes the three colors and then decides that he overdid it and needs some more white. Once he has the colors properly mixed he moves his brush to the canvas and with three subtle yet efficient circular strokes he creates the shape of a head at the top of the woman's body.

The head seems to be gazing out to sea, but it is hard to say without the features. Brother Small studies the poster for a moment then cleans his brush before dipping it into the brown paint. Then he moves to the canvas again, this time with the still hands of a surgeon he adds a light streak of brown over the eyes, then a small perpendicular shadow, which perfectly suggests the presence of a nose. He then adds two small shadows, which work together to create the lips. The face is there, but it still looks incomplete.

Brother Small sits back and then reaches for his palette again, this time he just barely touches the brush to the smattering of brown paint at the edge of the palette. He slowly lifts it towards the canvas, pauses for a moment and then adds a brown touch under the eyebrow, an eye. Now the face is complete, the woman is alive, connected to the world around her. Then he adds two streaks of pink to the woman's lips and sits back in his chair.

Brother Small has spent about three minutes on the face. He again looks back at the poster. The two people are now finished. He must touch up the boat and then paint the water, the sky and some more sand by eight o'clock this evening. In the next twelve minutes, Brother Small finishes the boat. It takes a little bit longer than he had expected, but all in all, his mind is at ease. He feels confident that he will be able to complete the painting by eight o'clock.

Soon, the *1812 Overture* draws to a triumphant close and the disc jockey comes back on.

"It is 8:30 on this cool Thursday morning, now we will check the traffic for those of you heading into the office on area roads." With that Brother Small dips his brush in the jar of turpentine, rinses it off in the sink and gets up to go down to his "office."

He begins work at 8:30, luckily he does not have much of a commute. He heads out of his studio, catches the elevator and hits B. Down to the basement.

He is a few minutes late today, and he just barely makes it before the rush of students in the passing period between the first and second periods of the day.

He is in his shop and ready to work by 8:35. Today, like most days, will be busy. A few minutes after he has begun work on the three broken desks sitting outside of his shop, someone knocks on Brother Small's door.

"Come in, Come in," he replies to the knocks.

A student enters; he is a senior. Brother Small knows that but he does not think he has ever met the young man. "What can I do for you?" he inquires. The kid, a tall freckled boy wearing an untucked plaid shirt and untied shoes, says, "Nothing, I just have a message for you from the Dean's office." With that he hands Brother Small a piece of paper and then spins around and struts out of the shop slamming the door shut on his way.

"Thank you," Brother Small calls as he begins to open the paper. The note from the Dean's secretary is hand written. It says,

> Brother Small,
> We have a student leaving school because of an illness.
> She locked her keys in her car. She is waiting in our office.
> Can you come up here and help her?
> Thank You,
> Joan

Brother Small folds up the note and puts it in his breast pocket. Then he walks down to the other end of his shop where he has a collection of long metal wires, slim jims and crowbars tucked into one of his storage racks. He pulls out a piece of the wire that has been bent into a hook at one end. Then he reaches over his workbench for his plaid flannel overshirt. He puts it on and leaves for the Dean's office with the piece of wire in his right hand. He leaves the door to the shop wide open. He walks up the stairs to the first floor and heads straight down the corridor. He peeks into the Dean's office and sees a red-haired girl sitting in the chair by the door with her head down.

Brother Small gestures towards her and asks Joan, the matriarchal secretary, if this is the girl. She nods affirmatively. "Are you locked out of your car, honey?" The little girl looks up and nods slightly. Her freckled face is pale. It looks like she really is sick and not just skipping out on a test. Her eyes look to be half closed as she stands up and reaches for her bag, but Brother Small picks it up for her. "I'll take it," he says. "You just take it easy." Then he opens the door and the two of them walk down the hall towards the back parking lot.

On the left is the skinny body of the eighty-year old six foot three Jesuit carrying the girl's schoolbag in one hand and the tool he will use to open her car in his other hand. On the right is the girl's body, tiny in comparison to his. As they walk towards the sunlit windows, her profile can be seen as she looks up towards him and smiles.

"If you've got a car you must be at least a junior."

"Yeah, I'm a junior."

"How do you like your classes so far?"

"Oh, they're good. I mean, I like them all, I guess. Well, maybe not biology. I am having a pretty hard time with biology. I don't know, a lot of the stuff is just so complicated, but I guess it's important."

"It's important if you want to be a doctor, but everything else is just as important. What about college? Have you started to think about college yet?"

"Not really. Well, sort of, I guess. My dad went to Notre Dame."

"Notre Dame?" Brother Small asks. "Where is Notre Dame?" She looks up at him trying to judge the sincerity of the question. She sees him trying to a repress a smile and they both laugh.

They leave through the north exit of the building. The girl's station wagon is parked towards the back of the lot. It is a cool but beautiful fall day. On their left a few students throw a Frisbee back and forth on the tattered grass of the quad. One student sits beneath a tree, bundled in a jacket with his face buried in a paperback. One hundred yards to the right, cars streak towards the city on the Edens Expressway.

Brother Small and Emily, whom he has invited to his Sunday art lessons, walk towards her car, an old blue station wagon with artificial wood paneling that is falling off of the doors. When they reach the car, a gentle wind blows through the trees and into the quadrangle. The wind rustles some of the leaves out of the trees and they fall slowly toward the ground. One falls from the tree above Emily's car and slowly makes its way towards the ground until the back of Brother Small's collar catches it and breaks its fall. It comes to rest there on the back of his neck until Brother Small reaches for it and brushes it away quickly.

Brother Small is standing at the passenger door forcing the wire in the space between the door and the frame of the car. Once he has the wire inside of the door, he maneuvers it so that he can grab the lock with the wire and pull it up, unlocking the car. He pushes and pulls on the wire, it takes him nearly a minute but he manages to unlock the door. He opens it and sets Emily's bag on the floor in front of the passenger seat, and then reaches across and opens the driver side door for her.

"There you go, honey," he says as he gets back out of the car. "Sorry it took so long."

"Thank you so much, Brother Small," the girl says as she slowly climbs into the car. "I really appreciate it."

"I enjoyed meeting you, Emily. I hope you feel better, but now you better be going. Get home and get some rest."

"Thank you."

The car rumbles to life, emitting a cloud of purple and black smoke. Emily backs out of her parking space using only the rearview mirror. Brother Small holds his breath until he sees that she has cleared all of the cars near her. She rolls down the window as she pulls past him. "Thanks again, Brother Small."

"My pleasure," he replies.

My pleasure. He means that; it is his greatest pleasure. Brother Small truly takes joy in helping people. It makes him happy; more than anything else in the world he likes to serve other people. What a selfless concept; one we seem so painfully unfamiliar with in this day and age.

The Small children with Grandpa Small in Ryan's Woods in August 1930. Back row, from left to right are Jack, Jim, Marge, Grandpa Small holding Bud, cousin Joe, cousin Neil. Front row, left to right are Marie, Helen and cousin Maureen.

Jim Small as graduate of St. Rita in 1940

**Jim and Otis Crumbie making their way back
to the submarine base at Pearl Harbor**

**Jim with Jim McDonough, a classmate of his
who was also stationed at Pearl Harbor**

Jim and Ethel Von Art,
a woman he dated throughout his stint as a sailor

Jim at his parent's south side home with his partner, Officer Joe Bernet

Jim and Don Verkler taking a break at Jack's restaurant located at 51st and Stony Island. This is the only existing shot of Jim in his police uniform.

Jim, at his sister Marge's wedding with cousin Neil in the background. A man given over to the vanities of the world?

Brother Small, taken soon after he reentered the Jesuits in 1953

:

Brother Small with some early artwork at West Baden College

A pastel seascape completed soon after Brother Small's return to the
Jesuits

Brother Small serving in the kitchen at the Jesuit novitiate in Milford, Ohio.

Brother Small after a good day hunting

**Brother Small before his ill-fated tree climbing, baby bird scavenging
expedition at West Baden College**

Brother Small with captured, befriended birds

Brother Small setting up for the Ramble circa 1985

Brother Small standing before his exhibit at the 2000 Ramble with
The O'Donoghue family, Tom, June and Catherine.

Brother Small painting recently in his studio.

Brother Small the art critic and teacher visiting Jane Carney's art students in Loyola's art studio.

Two great friends. Brother Small and Father Norman Harland, S.J.

4

To fight and not to heed the wounds,

The steady discipline of
intimate friendship with
Jesus results in men
becoming like him.
-Henry Emerson Fosdick

Brother Small heads straight back to his shop after helping Emily into her car. He spends the remainder of his morning fixing the three broken desks that have been stacked outside of his door. Somehow the bookrack has fallen off of one of these desks. Repairing this is a sizable project for Brother Small who must make two small welds to reattach the bookrack to the legs of the desk. He carts the desk down the hallway to the boiler room where the small welding machine is located. He spends forty-five minutes working on this desk alone.

By the time he finishes the last of the busted desks, it is 11:35, time for lunch. He is back in the Jesuit residence by 11:40. He goes to the kitchen, opens the refrigerator and pulls out a Tupperware container half-filled with cold meatloaf from last night's dinner. He puts a couple of pieces of meatloaf onto some white bread and pours himself a glass of milk. He does not turn the lights on; he just sits at the table near the window eating by himself and looking out over Laramie Avenue and into the neighborhood that surrounds Loyola. He gazes blankly out the window to the west, chewing meditatively and sipping milk. Then a crow lands on the windowsill and Brother Small snaps to attention. He wonders if it is one of his crows. He sets down what's left of his sandwich and leans forward in his seat and studies the crow intently for a few seconds before it takes flight.

Last May Brother Small was headed to a funeral in Lake Forest, a suburb 10 miles north of Wilmette. On the way there, while stopped at the intersection of Rte. 41 and Old Elm Rd., he noticed one crow fly out of a tree, and a moment later he saw a different one fly into the same tree. "I knew that there were babies in that nest because when both of the parents are hunting for food the babies are pretty far along," he explained. So, he marked the spot and decided to come back and take the baby birds from their nest on the following day. He drove up the next morning and pulled over at the same spot. He walked around in the evergreens until he found the nest, and then he climbed a few branches in the evergreen until he could see into the crows' nest. He had been right; there were four baby crows. Each one was small enough to fit into the palm of his hand, but he thought they were at least six or seven weeks old because they were already covered with short black feathers. Brother Small reached quickly into the nest and took the babies out one by one and then sat them all together in the front seat of his car.

"A lot of people tell me I shouldn't go around taking crows out of their nests. It doesn't bother my conscience at all though," he explained. "Crows, you see, are the biggest violators of other birds' nests. They steal other birds' babies and then tear them up and feed them to their own young. If I take them, then I can be sure their parents won't be raiding other nests."

He pulled away and drove back to Loyola leaving an empty nest behind. He talked to the four birds for the duration of the ride home. They were obviously scared, but he did his best to calm them down. "I wanted them to get used to the sound of my voice," he said. "I was talking to them in a baby voice, saying words like 'skookers.' I don't even know what it means. I made it up. It doesn't mean anything. I just wanted to make sure that they got used to the sound of my voice, so I was saying anything that came to mind." When they got back to school, he built a spacious cage out of wood and chicken wire for his new pets in his basement shop.

They were afraid of him at first. He knew they would eventually warm up to him though. He had brought baby crows into the shop a number of times before, and they were always a little hesitant at first. But, once they got hungry, the fear vanished. In a few days, they began to eat out of his hand and perch on his forearm. The four baby crows began to trust him. They welcomed him into the shop by shaking their heads and spreading their wings. But when anyone else came into the room, they became visibly flustered, even if they were in their cage.

Four months later, when the crows were fully-grown and healthy, Brother Small carried them upstairs one by one and freed them. The next morning he filled his pockets with birdseed, went outside and spread it around on the ground where he had let the birds go. Once he had emptied his pockets, he turned and walked slowly back towards the doors of the school. Just before he reached the door, he heard the flapping of wings. He turned back and saw one of the crows flying towards him. He extended his arm and the crow landed there. In a few seconds, the other three were circling around, and one of them landed on his shoulder. The other two landed on the ground near his feet and began to eat the birdseed he had left for them.

He stood there for a moment watching them eat, and then someone opened the door behind him and the birds were gone in a flutter of feathers and noise. Brother Small turned and saw the student who had intended to step outside and watch him feed the birds.

"I'm really sorry," the student said, holding the door open with his right hand.

"It's okay," Brother Small said as he turned back towards the school. "Maybe they will come back."

Every morning for the next three months, Brother Small filled his hands and pockets with birdseed and went outside to a quiet corner of the quadrangle. Three of the four birds continued to come to him every day and land either on his forearm or his shoulder. They would never hurt him. He was always gentle with them, and they were always gentle with him. Somehow they seemed to understand that he did not intend to harm them. They trusted him, with their lives really, but if anyone opened a nearby window or door they would scatter immediately, demonstrating that they were very much wild birds who had forged a relationship with just one human being.

Brother Small's relationship with birds began when he returned to the Jesuit novitiate forty-five years ago. He was fresh off the police force and he missed police work, especially the excitement of chasing and capturing criminals. When he arrived at Milford, he brought along a little bit of the police force: his guns. He and his close friend, Brother Bill Haas, used the guns to start hunting. They didn't have the time or the resources to go on long hunts for deer or rabbit, but they did have a pair of handguns and plenty of space around the grounds of the novitiate where they could hunt crows.

They continued to hunt when they were transferred to West Baden College where they spent weekend after weekend hiding in a wooden shed and shooting crows out of a nearby tree. They had a grand time. On a good day, they would shoot down three or four crows. They did not use the dead crows for anything. They just picked up their bodies and deposited them in the trash.

Brother Small and Brother Haas both became accomplished marksmen and could hit the medium-sized crows in the chest from 100 yards almost every single time. But they did occasionally miss and do permanent damage to the birds without actually killing them.

At first they killed these birds too, just to put them out of their misery, even though it meant they had to waste another bullet. But Brother Small eventually came up with the idea of saving the birds and keeping them alive so that they could be used as decoys.

He had tried to get babies out of a nest, but this plan backfired when he fell out of a tree, broke his back, spent three weeks in the hospital and lost tree-climbing privileges in his province. He was, needless to say, excited about the wounded birds, because he would finally have his decoys. The next time he found a wounded bird, he took it to a crude cage he had fashioned in his workshop in the basement of the main college building at West Baden.

Two weeks later, Brother Small successfully employed the bird as a decoy. He and Brother Haas had a career day, killing seven crows and wounding one more. Brother Small took the two wounded birds back down to his shop and fed them every day. Weeks later, when he entered the shop the two birds spread out their wings and rolled their eyes back in their head. Brother Small quickly came to understand this as a gesture of affection. He was amazed. These birds were able to recognize him, and they seemed to like him. "It's amazing," he says, mostly to himself, as he thinks back to that day.

Amazing or not, this did not immediately deter Brother Small from hunting crows. He and his buddies continued to hunt, and bring home more wounded birds. Before long, they had so many maimed and broken birds in the basement that they were encouraged by their superior to kill some of them. But Brother Small refused; he didn't explain himself, he just continued to take care of the birds.

He didn't quit hunting completely until he came up to Chicago in 1969. But as the years wore on, he rarely went out to hunt. He had lost interest in shooting the birds and had begun to direct his energy towards raising them. He began by taking care of the wounded birds he had been using as decoys. But he enjoyed raising them so much that when the wounded birds were gone, he resorted to taking baby crows out of their nests.

Since his days at West Baden, he has developed an affinity for all birds, not just crows. For the last ten years, he has had at least one pet bird, if not five or six living in his basement shop. Over time he has housed many types of birds: finches, parakeets, cockatiels, and even gigantic parrots. Most of these birds have been gifts of sorts from people who no longer wanted to take care of the birds they had once purchased as pets. Brother Small has also rescued some escaped domesticated birds from roadsides or from the quadrangle and brought them into his basement sanctuary. Each of these birds serves as a very simple and real reminder to Brother Small that God is in fact present in all things.

"When I started raising crows, I began to realize how each crow is different; every one is an individual. I'm not saying they are people, but you could see each one was different; each one had a different mind. And some of them were so wise. I could see God in those simple little creatures, and it amazed me because they are just one of thousands of types of animals, and I was able to see God in them."

This idea is hard for me to understand because I often don't see the good in people, much less the God in them, or in birds for that matter. In a crow, I see a potentially violent black bird. I am annoyed by pushy people and angered by inconsiderate people. I see faults in many people, not God. I was somewhat taken aback by the idea that Brother Small can see God in animals.

"How do you know that God is in these birds or at work in these birds?"

"Have you ever seen a bird's nest?" he replied. "Of course you have, but up close have you ever seen one? They're amazing. On the outside they are so rough. They're made up of twigs, sticks, bark, and pieces of thread. Inside they are as smooth as silk. Really it's like silk. It's beautiful. Well, who taught birds how to do that? The crows I raised built nests like that, and I surely didn't teach them how to do it. No human could, not even a brain surgeon. Well, someone has got to be helping them; God is working through them. God helps them build those nests, just like he helps me paint and he helps other humans build skyscrapers. There's no denying it."

"You like birds so much, do you think there was anything wrong with shooting crows for sport?"

"Well, today I do. I wouldn't go hunting now. I just feel differently about it now. I used to just walk around looking for crows so that I could shoot them just for fun. Now, I wouldn't want to hurt them. I don't even like to see them hurting each other. They are God's creatures. Hunting is still a sport, though, and I don't fault anyone who does it. I did it, and it was fun and exciting, but I just feel differently about life now; every life is worth taking care of."

"Have you changed as a person much since you have been a Jesuit?"

"I have changed over time. Not just in terms of hunting, but in a lot of things. But, to be honest, it's hard for me to know how I have changed; it would be easier for other people to tell you whether or not I have changed. I do know that I love people much more now than I ever did before. I've learned to try to look at the bright side of things, especially people. Everybody is good. There is something good about everyone we know, even the people who are not our favorites, and there is something bad about everyone we know, even the people who are our favorites. But why dwell on it? Since I have joined the Jesuits, I have done a better job of looking at the bright side. A lot of times, I see God in people, and I see people as God's creations, and that really affects the way that I think of people. How would I treat the bum on the street if I knew he was Christ in disguise? Probably a lot differently than I do now. So, I try to think that way. I've changed to thinking that way; I'm not very good at it yet though."

Brother Small's workday, like most people's, is divided by lunch. Meal times tend to a play a large role in all of our schedules. Lunch is important physically, as a refueling period, but also as a social time. Lunch gives everyone at least a couple minutes to eat, possibly sit down, relax and talk about the day, what has happened, and what lies ahead for the afternoon. Our lives revolve around food because we, quite simply, cannot live without it.

Each meal in Brother Small's day is accompanied by a prayer session. Man, after all, cannot live on bread alone. The old adage is true for Brother Small. His prayer sessions are just as important to him as his meals. His body cannot survive without food. His spirituality is no different. It cannot survive, much less flourish without prayer, and he definitely cannot survive, much less thrive, without his spirituality.

Once he finishes his meatloaf sandwich he heads to his bedroom where he once again prays. He structures his afternoon prayer differently than his morning prayer. He focuses more directly on the events of his day, both the good and the bad. This particular exercise, the examen or examination of conscience, is a central element of Jesuit spirituality.

Brother Small begins his third prayer session of the day by trying to bring himself into the presence of God, just as he did this morning. Sometimes this is difficult; sometimes it comes easily. But in order to do it, Brother Small must focus his attention and vision on the presence of God in his life, particularly God's presence at that moment. In other words, he must stop thinking about himself, his needs and his desires. For a moment he must not think about Mrs. Ryan's painting or about the fact that he has had a persistent ache in his stomach since breakfast this morning. Instead he must think about God, how God is present in his world and present in his life.

This afternoon he envisions himself at the crucifixion of Christ. He kneels in front of the cross, and Christ's body hangs before him, nails protruding from the wrists and ankles. Blood runs from the cuts on his forehead down over his face and into his thick beard. Brother Small studies the image in his mind, and by doing so, he is able to break from the events of the day.

Once he has successfully put himself in God's presence, he begins his afternoon examination, which consists of five major points or ideas.

First, he gives thanks for all that God has done for him and for humankind. Today he thanks God for the opportunity to work at Loyola and to get to know so many wonderful people. He thanks God for introducing him to Emily. He gives thanks for his body, which he feels is remarkably healthy for a man his age. He gives thanks for the meals he's enjoyed so far today, corn flakes and leftover meatloaf.

In the second part of his afternoon prayer, he asks the Holy Spirit to shed light on the events of his day, particularly on his actions, so that he may better understand them, both the good ones and the bad ones. He asks God to help him see his own faults.

This fascinates me for two reasons. First of all, Brother Small wants to know his faults. I think most people are afraid of their faults. Secondly, he realizes he cannot understand his faults on his own; he just cannot see all of them. He knows he needs God's help.

In the third part of the prayer, he examines everything he has done that day. He considers his virtuous thoughts, emotions and actions as well as the negative thoughts, feelings, and deeds. He asks himself why he has done them and tries to understand what has motivated him to behave in these different ways.

In the fourth part, he sincerely asks for forgiveness for each of the negative aspects of his day. He admits to himself and to God that the way he has lived this morning has left something to be desired.

In the fifth section of the prayer, he prays that God will help him to be more virtuous. He wants to live a better life, he wants to be a better person, he wants to love more, and he asks God to help him do this. He asks God to give him strength to be a soldier of Christ. He prays that he can fight to be more like Christ. In some ways it is like a battle. Each day he fights to imitate Christ in a world that oftentimes scorns those who strive to follow Him and scoffs at actions motivated by love for God.

The idea of striving to emulate Jesus is at the center of Jesuit theology, as well as the Jesuit approach to education and life. It is easy to talk about emulating Christ or to verbally commit one's life to this idea. But, to actually try and do it each and every day can be difficult and sometimes exhausting work. Like any other life-defining task, it requires preparation, hard work, dedication and concentration. This is Brother Jim Small's work. He is a Jesuit. He tries to live like Christ did. He tries to bring light to the world so that others may be able to see and understand God's presence in their lives and in the world.

He kneels before his desk while he does his examination. Seeing him there, I must be honest, I find myself wondering what he could actually be thinking about. What in his conscience even needs to be examined? What could he have possibly done wrong this morning? Nothing, right? He got up early, prayed, worked, painted, and now he is praying again. I sincerely wonder what sins he could be confessing, or examining as he kneels quietly before his desk. So I ask him, "What are your greatest faults?"

"Greatest faults. Well, that'd take me a long time to go through that, I've got so many of them. One would definitely be not showing enough interest in other people. A lot of times, when I am introduced to people, I don't pay attention to their name, and then the next time I see them I can't remember their name, because I didn't pay attention. It's not that I didn't hear it, it's just that I didn't pay attention. I figure I'll never meet them again, but I do meet them and then I can't remember their name. And I can see how it makes people feel bad sometimes when I cannot remember their names because it seems like I don't care. That's just a slight fault, but it's definitely a fault. The worst part is that I never really try to overcome that.

Another fault of mine is that I am not a good worker; my work ethic is not very good, you know. There's a lot more I could do that I don't do, and if I had my life to do over again, I'd try to do a lot more than I ever did, to try to help people.

Another fault is that when I visit people in the hospital, I find it hard to empathize with them. I have a feeling that I want to get out of that room ASAP instead of staying there and trying to help them. It's so hard for me to see people suffer when I can't do anything about it. That's a fault; I know that. I took care of patients for years and I always found it hard when patients were vomiting or sick in any way to be with them, and yet it was my job to be with them. That was a fault."

"Do you think finding it difficult is a fault?"

"Well, you should overcome it."

"You did. Didn't you?"

"I had to; it was my job, but I still felt as though I'd rather not be there. The people who took care of the lepers, they loved doing that, but I was just there doing it because I had to. What else? As far as faults are concerned, you ask anybody, and they'll go down the list of all of my faults. Most of the time, we don't even know our own faults. We spend so much time talking about other people's faults, we end up being totally unaware of our own faults, and we are always surprised when somebody notices a fault of ours."

"How do you try to overcome your faults?"

"Through prayer and confession. First of all, I try to realize I am a sinner, and once I have done that, I can try to overcome it and do better. But I have to realize I can't do it alone, I need the help of the Lord. But, the biggest thing is seeing what I'm doing wrong or being aware of it, and I do this by examining my conscience. You know, if you don't know what you're doing wrong, then you can't do anything to make it better, and it's easy to go through life without paying attention to that, but I've found that that's how I do better in life."

Once he has finished examining his conscience, he moves to his chair, where he takes one of his few breaks of the day. He leaves his glasses on the desk, closes his eyes and bows his head. His hands are folded in his lap and his feet are planted firmly on the floor. He sleeps peacefully for about thirteen minutes and then wakes up suddenly. He stands up, retrieves his glasses and walks out the door. He winds his way back to his workshop, through the multitude of students in the dark corridors of Loyola's cavernous basement.

As he nears the doors to his shop, two tall boys, basketball players maybe, call out, "What's up, Brother Small?"

"Hi fellas."

As he reaches to open the door to his shop, Brother Small notices a young woman making her way slowly down the hallway. She has braces on her teeth, and they protrude from her small mouth and practically jump off of her freckled face. She has big bulky braces on her legs as well, and she does not seem sure of herself as she shuffles down the corridor. She looks as if she might tumble over at any minute. She holds her right hand up the whole time and her little finger dances across the painted cinder block wall as she moves slowly forward. Twice she loses her balance a little bit and leans on her hand to right herself.

Behind Brother Small students look away from her, avoiding eye contact. They talk to their friends, or if they're alone they look at their watches or just lower their heads. The shuffler, too, bows her head and she does not see Brother Small as she plods ungracefully towards him.

"Hi, honey," he says endearingly. "Where have you been? I haven't seen you around here in a while."

She looks up and her face breaks into a wide smile, momentarily outshining the braces, which still stick out of her mouth. Then her pale face blushes to a deep shade of red behind the thick freckles. She continues to smile, lowers her head again and shuffles onward. Brother Small opens the door and enters his shop.

I don't know if he knew that girl, and to be honest I don't care, because it doesn't matter. Most people see her as a girl with braces, a limp, and a handicap. They hear the noise she makes as she shuffles slowly through her day. Brother Small, on the other hand, sees a person; he doesn't see the braces on her teeth or the ones that keep her fragile legs from collapsing. He doesn't hear her shuffle or notice how slowly she walks. He sees a person there. He doesn't look through her or look away because she doesn't make him uncomfortable. He looks right into her eyes, maybe even into her soul, and says, "Where have you been? I haven't seen you around here in a while."

I don't know what this meant to her. I can't be sure but, judging from the smile that brightened her face and her blushing cheeks, she was flattered, and she was happy. He had given her something very simple. He hadn't looked away, like so many people do. He hadn't seen through her. Did this give her hope? I don't know for sure, but I bet it did. Did it make her happy? Did it make her day? Did it remind her that she, too, is important? I can't say for sure, but having seen the smile on her face, I have a feeling it did.

How many times has Brother Small done this? I don't have an answer for this either. But there must be hundreds of people like this girl who have had their days brightened by this friendly old man who just takes the time and makes the effort to treat them with dignity and love, to treat them like human beings and children of God.

Brother Small's close friend, Brother Haas, commented on Brother Small's way with people, and his comments help explain what motivates these tiny little acts of profound kindness. He said, "He's close to God, you see. He sees God in all people and all things. I think that's why he's so interested in . . . well, anybody really, but especially in the people who need more attention, sympathetic attention usually. There are those who aren't too gifted, in sports, academics or personality. One way or another he always seems to take to those people."

The small story of the shuffling girl is emblematic of Brother Jim Small's life. It is a simple, seemingly insignificant encounter. But, it has made a difference in someone's life.

He has a busy afternoon of work ahead. A week ago he promised one of the Loyola teachers, Phil Nieman, a former horse jockey, a framed painting of a racehorse by week's end. He also promised Mrs. Sheila Brookman, who works in the Admissions Office, a frame for a portrait he had done of her daughter. The portrait turned out very nicely; it is big, bigger than any he has done recently.

While it is big, it is certainly not his biggest. The largest is probably the one he did of Abraham Lincoln. One of Brother Small's friends, Roger Hickey, asked him to do the portrait for his father's eightieth birthday. Brother Small obliged and painted a huge reproduction of a famous portrait of Lincoln. It turned out that the portrait was too big, and Roger Hickey has since loaned it to Peter Fitzgerald, a Republican senator from Illinois. The picture is presently hanging in Fitzgerald's office in Washington, DC, where it serves as a backdrop for all of the television interviews that take place in his office.

As soon as he enters his shop, he flips on the radio. The radio he keeps in his shop is old, really old. It has been down in his shop for over ten years. It shows, too. It is covered with drops of different color paint and a thick layer of dust. It is scratched and dented and worn. The stations don't always come in perfectly but with a little bit of work Brother Small manages to get a clear signal from one of Chicago's FM classical musical stations.

Satisfied, he walks over to the back of his workshop where he keeps two large racks, both full of a wide assortment of framing molding. Some of the pieces are long; some of them are short; some ornate and some very plain.

He digs through the rack for a minute or so until he finds what he thinks is the perfect piece of wood. He pulls out this seven-foot section and carries it over to his table saw. This whole time the radio has been playing commercials.

He measures and cuts the horizontal sides of the frame for the portrait of Mrs. Brookman's daughter. He measures the width of the portrait with a fold out ruler and then marks that distance on the wood and cuts accordingly. His hands work quickly and carefully, running the wood firmly over the rapidly spinning saw blade.

He flips the pieces of the frame over and places a small piece of extra wood over each of the four joints and then taps nails into each side of the extra piece of wood. The nails hold each of the four pieces of the frame together.

The radio continues to play in the background, and an item from a recap of the morning's news catches Brother Small's attention.

"A municipal worker has been admitted to St. Anthony's Hospital after falling twenty feet from a tree branch onto the 2700 block of South Kostner. Doctor Mitchell Byrne, the attending physician, commented, 'The patient does not seem to have sustained any major injuries, miraculously nothing in his neck or back is broken.' That is all the news, after these messages we will have the Boston Symphony Orchestra performing Beethoven's symphony # 7 in A major presto."

Brother Small has not fallen out of a tree in a long time. He probably would have but when he was at West Baden College, before he came to Loyola, his Jesuit provincial suspended his tree climbing privileges after he had a fall much like the man now at St. Anthony's Hospital. In 1958 Brother Small explained his idea of stealing baby crows from their nests and using them as hunting decoys to Brother Haas.

"How in the deuces, do you plan on getting up to the nests of these birds?" Brother Haas asked when he heard the plan.

"Easy. I'm just going to climb the trees. I climbed trees all the time when I was a little kid."

"If you're going to climb, you oughta use the old set of climbers I've got. It's a set of climbers my dad used to climb poles in World War I. There's spikes for both of your shoes, and a leather belt that goes around your waist and around the tree. So you lean back on the belt and then use the spikes on the shoes to climb up the tree."

Brother Small took him up on the offer. A couple days later he set out in search of baby crows. He put the climbers in the front seat of the car and then drove the country roads around the college. After about forty-five minutes, he spotted a crow slowly descending into its nest. He immediately pulled the car over and waited for the crow to leave. Once it left the nest, he hurried to the bottom of the tree and pulled the metal climbing spikes onto his leather shoes. Then he wrapped the leather belt around the back of the tree and across his lower back, fastened it, and began to climb the tree.

He climbed slowly at first as he acquainted himself with the equipment. But soon he got a feel for the spikes and the way they bit into the wood, and his tentative steps slowly extended themselves into longer more aggressive ones. After fifteen minutes of rigorous climbing, he found himself thirty-five feet off the ground peering into an empty crow's nest.

Disappointed, he began his descent. About six feet below the nest, he encountered the first branch of his downward climb. He had done pretty well on the branches on the way up, but it was scarier going down. The branches presented an obstacle because he could not get the safety belt past any of them without taking it off, climbing beyond the branch and then reattaching it. So, once he approached the first branch, Brother Small kicked his spikes into the tree bark and unfastened the belt. He looked down and realized that he was nearly thirty feet off the ground.

Once he had the belt unfastened he placed it between his legs and then reached his arms around the tree. He had to climb down two or three feet so that he could get past the large branch and reattach his belt. He pulled out one of his spiked shoes, slid it farther down the trunk of the tree and then kicked it back in to the wood. Unfortunately he also kicked it through the middle of the belt.

He moved his other foot down and set it in the tree so that his two feet were even with each other. Then he pulled his right foot, which had spiked the belt back out of the tree trunk. He began to shake his foot violently trying to get the belt loose, and as he shook it, the other foot began to lose its hold in the tree. He did not notice this, and when he leaned down, to try to pull the belt off his foot, the left foothold gave way and he tumbled more than twenty-five feet to the ground.

He can't remember if he was knocked out or not, but he does recall lying on the ground in great pain for quite some time before even trying to move. When he did move he managed to right himself and walk slowly through the woods back to the car. He drove back to West Baden, and when he arrived he did not even try to get out of the car. He just parked at the loading docks and began to call out the window for someone to help him. Three Jesuits came to his aid and drove him immediately to the hospital. He had broken his back in two places.

"Brother Small, you had this very literal fall early in your career, but have you had any figurative falls, times when you were down and struggled to get up?"

"Well, in a way, yes. There have certainly been times when my spirituality has been at a low ebb. During those times I didn't want to pray, I didn't want to go to Mass, I just didn't have it in me. And it was hard. It's as hard as anything else I've dealt with in my time as a Jesuit. I know those periods are temptations, and all I could do was try not to be tempted, continue to pray, and weather the storm. Eventually I got it back. And I needed it; losing your ability to walk for a while is bad, but losing your vitality and your spirit is awful, much worse than being laid up in a hospital."

Brother Small's tree mishap was not his only fall. The second one is much more recent; it happened at Loyola in 1985. This time Brother

Small was hunting for gold, not birds. In years past Brother Small fashioned the nameplates for all of his paintings by hand. He had the engraving machine in his shop, but the gold plates were sometimes hard to come by. He ordered them regularly, but he painted and framed so much stuff that he would run out of plates long before he got a chance to order new ones. When he was really in a bind and needed some plates fast, he would hunt around the school for old ones.

On this particular afternoon, he had planned on rummaging through the storage rooms high above Loyola's gym balcony. Many of the school's athletic teams' old trophies were stored up there, and Brother Small planned on pirating some of the name plates from the trophies, flipping them over and using them as name plates for his paintings.

He managed to find a ladder tall enough to reach the storage room, which was twenty feet above the painted cement floor. He carried the ladder up to the balcony, leaned it against the wall, and began climbing. He was one step away from reaching the door into the storage room when he felt the ladder slip. He stopped and held himself perfectly still hoping the legs would hold long enough for him to make the last step, but as soon as he shifted his weight again, the ladder lost its hold on the cement floor and slid out from under him. He fell eighteen feet, landing on the ladder and pavement.

He couldn't move. He just waited, lying on the floor of the gym balcony for someone to come and discover him. After about half an hour, one of his coworkers found him and helped him back to his feet. He had a difficult time standing. His hip was in great pain, and he could not walk.

Two of the Jesuit priests at Loyola took him to the hospital to have his hip examined. The doctor examined the hip and then decided to take some x-rays. A few minutes after he took the pictures, the doctor came back into the room, held up the x-rays and asked, "Who is shooting at you Brother?"

"Shooting at me?" Brother Small asked, somewhat taken aback by the question. "I don't think anybody. I guess if anyone is, it must be the students," he said, chuckling slightly.

Then the doctor pointed to the x-ray, handed it to Brother Small who was lying awkwardly in the hospital bed and said, "Somebody has, there is a bullet lodged in your hipbone." Sure enough, there was a black bullet right there in his hip. Brother Small's mind immediately began reviewing the events of his life, trying to figure out when he could have possibly been shot. It couldn't have happened recently. He hadn't hunted for years, and to his knowledge none of the students around school did any shooting.

He had never really been shot at in the police force, except for that night at the wedding reception, when the little bomb exploded. Later that night he and Joe Bernet had inspected the homemade bomb and discovered that it had been made out of six shells from a twenty-two-caliber pistol. "Amazing nobody was killed," Joe said at that time. "Yeah, nobody was even hit," Jim added. But he was wrong.

By the time Beethoven's piece rolls to an end, Brother Small has completed the frame for the portrait. He places the painting inside the completed frame. It fits tightly. He fishes in his breast pocket and finds a crumpled up napkin. The night before, while painting in his studio, he scribbled down the measurements of Mr. Ryan's painting. Luckily he has the same shirt on today and the napkin is intact. He studies the measurements and then begins to build the frame for Mr. Ryan's painting. He had told Mr. Ryan that he might not have time to frame the painting. But, he has twenty minutes to spend building the frame this afternoon. That way, when he finishes the painting later this evening, he will be able to just slide it into the frame and give it to Mr. Ryan complete.

Once he's completed all three frames, Brother Small reaches under his workbench, without skipping a beat, and pulls out a small clear plastic box. He opens the box and takes out twelve identical pieces of wood, each of them about three and a half inches long. In the next fifteen to twenty minutes, he will fashion these twelve pieces of wood into six wooden crosses. Then he will drill a hole into the top of each cross and run a brown string through it so that it can be worn around someone's neck or carried. The crosses will be used for the Kairos retreat, which ends tomorrow.

He cuts the crosspieces and then carves identical notches into every piece of wood so that he can fit them together. One by one he glues the two pieces of wood together and then puts all six of the completed crosses into a wood clamp to hold them for a few minutes while the glue dries.

Once the glue on the first cross seems dry, he picks it up and drills a hole in the top. Then he runs one of the strings though the hole and ties it off. He picks up the second cross and does the same thing.

At the same time, Tim Sassen, one of the school's chemistry teachers and technology consultants, walks quickly out of the computer lab down the hall and heads for the cafeteria, which is about to close for the day.

Brother Small picks up the third cross and drills the hole. He picks up the fourth cross, but just as he is about to begin drilling he drops it. It bounces off the drill, which he's holding in his right hand. He catches it when it is still right next to the drill, but in the process he gets the skin between his index finger and his thumb on his left hand caught in between the spinning metal piece, and the plastic shell of the drill. Unfortunately he also hit the trigger of the drill and it spun for just a second. And in that second it cut the skin and pulled a lot of it up inside the drill.

He doesn't yell or even grimace. He holds still and grinds his teeth. He's stuck because he can't walk away from the drill; it hangs from a chain that is attached to the pipes in the ceiling of his shop. He can't let go of the drill to try to free his hand, because he knows it will hurt to have the weight of the drill hanging from the skin on his hand.

So he stands quietly in his shop as the blood begins to run down his hand, then he sees Mr. Sassen walking past the shop in the hallway. "Excuse me?" Brother Small calls, but he seems to have missed Mr. Sassen who was already past the door when he called his name.

Then Mr. Sassen reappears, walking backwards, so that he can see Brother Small. "Were you calling me?"

"Yes, I was" Brother Small says peering over his glasses, which slipped down on his nose while he was inspecting his hand. Mr. Sassen walks in to the shop; he doesn't know Brother Small very well, but he seems willing to help.

"What can I do you for?" he asks smiling. Then Brother Small picks up his hand and shows Mr. Sassen, saying, "I just need you to hold the drill while I undo this piece here and get my hand back out."

"Okay, no problem," Mr. Sassen says as he grabs the drill, then he continues, "If this had happened to me I would've been running up and down the halls screaming CALL 911, CALL 911! Why didn't you come get help?"

"The drill's connected to the pipes," Brother Small says, pointing to the chain holding the drill. As soon as he says this, he pulls his hand back out of the drill. There is a lot of blood and a deep cut. Some of the skin has been removed, and the rest is bunched up at one end of the gash. Brother Small pulls this piece of skin off and thanks Mr. Sassen for his help.

Mr. Sassen leaves, still hoping to get to the cafeteria, but he probably will end up missing it. Once he's gone, Brother Small picks up the drill and drills the remaining three holes in the crosses. He carefully threads the strings through each of the six holes. He ties every string into a knot, and then sets the completed crosses on the end of his workbench.

Once he's done that, he walks across the hall to the boys' locker room and rinses off his hand.

5

To toil and not to seek for rest

The highest reward for a man's
toil is not what he gets for it,
but what he becomes by it.

-John Ruskin

Brother Small leaves the boys locker room with a paper towel wrapped around the wound on his hand. On the way back to his workshop he spots Coach Rick Miller, the head wrestling coach, who is making his way down the stairs towards the locker room.

"Rick, congratulations on your new baby," Brother Small says as he extends his hand. "I've been meaning to stop by and congratulate you. This is the first girl, right, and her name is Nicole?"

Coach Miller replies quickly, smiling broadly, "That's right, Brother, the first girl, Nicole, and she is a beautiful, beautiful little girl."

Coach Miller has four children: Cory, Connor, Ryan, all boys, and Nicole, his first daughter. He lives in Woodridge, which is quite a distance from Loyola, at least a forty-five-minute drive, but with traffic it usually takes an hour. Because he lives so far away, Coach Miller's kids rarely get to come with him to school.

Seven years ago when his first son, Cory, was just two, Coach Miller brought him into school. One way or another, they bumped into Brother Small who invited the two of them into his shop to see his pet birds. The next time they came to Loyola, Cory asked over and over, "Daddy, can we see the birds?" He learned Brother Small's name on his second visit, and every time he has returned to Loyola, he has asked to go see Brother Small. His younger brothers share the same enthusiasm for the man and his birds.

"It's amazing," says Coach Miller. "Because we live so far away, they've

The Small Things

probably only been to Loyola six or seven times, and he has remembered their names every single time. He even knew my daughter's name, and he has never seen her before."

He loves children, and he welcomes them into his life all the time. Children somehow understand his love for them because they are comfortable around him. Somehow he reaches them and sets them at ease.

"He has an aura," says Coach Miller. "It's like he has this power over people. Well, power isn't the right word; it's more of an acceptance and understanding of people."

Sometimes understanding and accepting people can be the most powerful actions in the world. Brother Small has been doing it his entire life. Coach Miller, not surprisingly, is one of many who have found that his children have developed a special affection for Brother Small.

Joe Taylor, who coordinates many of the activities in Loyola's ministry office, has had similar experiences throughout his thirty-four years at Loyola. His office is located down in the basement of the school, right next to Brother Small's shop. Mr. Taylor has seven children. He lives in Palatine, a thirty-minute drive from Loyola, but his family pediatrician was situated in the Old Orchard Shopping Center, located just minutes from the school. In years past, Mr. Taylor and his wife Audrey, who also works in the ministry office, would bring their kids over to Loyola if they happened to have a doctor's appointment in the middle of the day.

"You wouldn't see Brother Small for days; he's so busy, you know. And then as soon as we had the kids in here he would appear. It was almost like he could smell kids." Whether he can smell them or not, Brother Small is certainly drawn to little children, and no matter who they are, they seem to like him. According to Mr. Taylor, "He's one of the few people who has been able to pick up our children without them crying. At least five of them have been in here with him, and all of them were the same way."

145

3-KEAR

G. R. Kearney

It is ten minutes past two when Brother Small returns to his shop. He shuts off the lights, turns off the radio and closes the door to his shop, though he doesn't lock it. He walks hurriedly up to his room in the Jesuit residence. He bandages his hand and then takes off his work clothes, folding them neatly. He replaces those clothes with his clerics: a black shirt, black pants and a Roman collar.

For the last month, despite the fact that he has been very busy, he has left school every afternoon to visit Father Norm Harland, SJ, who is recovering from a complicated surgery that removed a malignant tumor from his esophagus.

Looking back on his extended illness and recuperation, Father Harland said, "Brother Small was the safety net; he was there when everything and everyone else failed. I knew he would be there for me. And he was there, always with such grace, cheer and wit."

Brother Small is the prefect of health care in Loyola's Jesuit community. He worked for three years as an infirmarian at West Baden College early in his Jesuit career. He is the most qualified to be the community health prefect. It is not, however, his past experience in the medical field that has made him good at this job, but rather his gentle way of dealing with people, his generosity and his unending patience. His responsibilities as the prefect of health care are to drive the Jesuits in the community to their doctor's appointments and to pick up their prescriptions. His ultimate function is to be a companion to any sick Jesuit in the community while he struggles to recuperate and get back to his normal life.

In early November of 1998, Father Harland called on Brother Small. "Jim, I've got a doctor's appointment. I've been having some pain in my chest, and I've had a hard time swallowing lately. So I made an appointment to get it checked out. Would you mind going over there with me? I'd like to have you there in case I get any bad news." And so began their six-month journey together. Brother Small drove Father Harland to the doctor's office on the day of his appointment. "Jim, I'll call you up here if I need you, okay?" Father Norm said as he shut the car door and trudged into the hospital. Brother Small waited in the car.

An hour later, the two of them sat before the doctor awaiting the diagnosis. "I wanted him up there, as soon as I knew I would be hearing bad news. I was worried that I wouldn't understand the seriousness of it. Either I would think it was much more or much less serious than it actually was. Jim would know. And I knew he would take the news calmly."

The doctor sat behind his desk. He hesitated for a moment as he looked at these two silver-haired Jesuits. Then he began to speak, "Father Norm, the tests show a tumor on your esophagus . . . Only 40% with this type of cancer survive . . . The tumor is growing; it needs immediate attention . . . We'll assemble a medical treatment team today . . . A week from now, you'll begin chemotherapy and radiation . . . In three months we'll perform surgery to remove the remains of the tumor from your esophagus."

Brother Small drove Father Norm to the hospital a week later to begin the first of his twenty-five radiation treatments. At first the radiation had little effect on his body. He felt nothing, though the doctor assured him that the tumor was shrinking. The short-term effect of the treatment proved not to be entirely positive. The radiation began to burn away much of the healthy flesh in Father Harland's throat and the inner wall of his esophagus. After two weeks, the pain was so bad that he could barely swallow.

Father Norm lived at Loyola during his radiation and chemotherapy treatment. But, when the pain in his throat became so bad, he was admitted into the hospital. The doctors inserted a feeding tube, but his system rejected it. He soon returned to Loyola where Brother Small worked diligently as his personal caretaker. He continued to drive Father Norm to and from his treatments. When he became sick and tired, Brother Small brought him soft, easy-to-swallow food. He fed him. He helped him bathe.

On February 11, 1999, two days before his surgery, Father Norm walked Brother Small through his bedroom showing him where everything was, just in case he did not live through the surgery. The next day, the team of doctors from the Evanston Northwestern Hospital performed surgery on Father Norm. They removed the tumor and a large section of the esophagus that had surrounded the tumor.

The surgery went well, but post-operative complications abounded. The sutures in Father Norm's esophagus did not hold, and it began to leak. Fortunately the discharge came out of his neck, rather than into his chest cavity, where it almost surely would have led to his death. He was forced to remain in the hospital for a month so that the doctors could monitor his recovery and prevent any more complications that would have put his extremely fragile, infection-prone body in great danger.

Father Norm spent a month in the hospital. Brother Small visited him every day, except one, when Father Norm called him and asked him not to come, "I'm just too tired to have anybody in here today Jim." Brother Small made it a point not to visit during the busy times when Father Norm's room was swamped with visitors, but rather during the times when he was stuck in the hospital by himself. He usually stayed for an hour, though sometimes he would remain there for two.

The two of them talked about Loyola, the teachers, the Jesuits, the athletes. They prayed. Occasionally they both napped. Looking back on their month together, Father Norm says, "He never tried to drive the pain away with silly, meaningless conversation. Rather he sat with me, and shared it with me, silently, like a great friend would. In that time he became one of my greatest friends."

Eventually Father Norm came home to his room at Loyola. He was nowhere near fully recovered. He spent the first few weeks of his time at Loyola in bed. He could not yet eat and took nourishment through a feeding tube. His body was fragile, susceptible always to the threat of infection. Brother Small acted as the primary caregiver and best friend during these weeks at Loyola. He visited Father Norm's room at least twice a day to change the feeding tube, disinfect the incision and change the bedding.

As Father Norm's condition slowly improved and he was able to move about and eat solid foods, he got the urge to see his friends. On many occasions, he went out for lunch or dinner with people he had not seen since he entered the hospital. He did not feel comfortable making these trips by himself so he took Brother Small. On several occasions, Brother Small drove Father Norm to a neighborhood lunch restaurant to meet his friends. Brother Small would stay for lunch. But he would always end up sitting idly by, listening patiently to conversation about people and places he did not know. He never complained. He went to lunch every single time Father Norm asked him.

When Brother Small arrives at the hospital on this particular day, Father Norm already has a visitor and the two of them are involved in a loud and quickly-moving conversation. Brother Small smiles at the visitor, bows his head and walks quietly past the vast display of flowers to the window. He takes his hat off but leaves his jacket on. He leans on the windowsill and peers out into suburban Evanston, looking down streets and through backyards.

When Father Norm's visitor is gone, Brother Small pulls a chair up to the bed. He reaches over the metal bed frame and rubs Father Norm's shoulder. "How's it going today, Norm?"

"Not bad. I feel better than I did yesterday, but there is still a lot of pain."

"I think you'll have pain like that for some time to come," Brother Small says as he removes his hand and sits back in his chair. The two of them remain there silently. Within minutes, Father Norm has fallen asleep. He sleeps for nearly forty-five minutes. Today Brother Small does not sleep. He sits next to Father Norm's bed with his hands folded and his eyes resting on his fellow Jesuit's rising and falling chest. Fifty minutes later, Father Norm rolls over in his bed, putting a strain on his feeding tube that awakens him. He rolls onto his back and glances at Brother Small.

"What time is it, Jim?"

"Oh, it's about ten minutes to four."

"Why don't you get out of here? I think I'll just sleep for the rest of the afternoon. Thanks for coming in."

"I'll see you tomorrow."

"There were days we talked and days we didn't," Father Norm says, recalling his stay in the hospital. "Either way, Jim was always there. He'd wear his clerics, his nice clothes, and he'd tell me about school, the funny stories and even some of the gossip. He would let me talk about the pain and the illness. The things I told him were awful, but he always listened. It was a wonderful opportunity for me to tell someone how I was feeling. He gave me so much optimism and cheer. The people in the hospital could see this. I was a different person when he left every day. He made me a better person, and he helped me get through that illness."

This loving care is not reserved only for Brother Small's Jesuit brothers. When his sister Marge, who lives on the far south side of Chicago, was released from the hospital after falling and breaking her hip in 1997, Brother Small immediately packed up his belongings and moved into her apartment to help her recuperate.

Each year Brother Small and the rest of the Jesuits at Loyola get two weeks of vacation time. "I usually don't take a vacation," Brother Small said. "Some of the guys do, but they just go somewhere, stay in a motel, take walks and watch TV. I can do all that stuff here."

But, in 1997, he used his time off to help nurture his sister back to health and take care of the chores around the house while she got her feet back on the ground. He still rose early in the morning. Every day he went to mass. But he did not have the same volume of work that he had back at Loyola. So he spent the extra time painting a number of pictures that were eventually sold in Loyola's spring fundraiser, The Ramble.

At 4:15 P.M. as Brother Small pulls back into the garage at Loyola, Chad Wickham and Tracey Gold climb quietly to the top of a remote stairwell that connects the basement to the second floor on the west side of the school. The stairs rise beyond the second floor, but there is nothing on the third floor except a locked maintenance closet. The door there has been bolted shut for years. Since the school opened its doors to women, the vacant landing has become a popular hangout for impatient students who find themselves unable to resist the temptation to kiss one another in school. Chad, a senior, and Tracey, a sophomore, are climbing the stairs to the dusty landing where they will lock lips for a few precious minutes until they must return to their work in the yearbook office.

Brother Small makes his way from the garage towards the Jesuit residence, by way of the elevator in the north end of the building. As the elevator lifts him from the first floor, he remembers an errand he had forgotten to do this afternoon. He reaches out and hits the button for the second floor.

Earlier today, probably some time during lunch, Thomas Fitzgerald, an English teacher at Loyola, left a message on Brother Small's voicemail. Apparently one of the windows in his classroom would not close properly. He said it was "no skin off my back" if the students dealt with the cold for a little while, but it should probably be fixed before the winter weather really set in.

Brother Small walked out of the elevator and made his way towards the door that led through the seldom-used stairwell where Chad and Tracey were kissing.

"Tracey, I love you so much, I mean . . . I love you."

"I love you too." With that Chad reached for her chin and began to kiss her. Chad had one hand on Tracey's cheek and the other in her dyed blonde hair when the door below them opened. They both froze. Their eyes, which had been closed, snapped open. Chad held Tracey's face in his hands. They had stopped kissing, and turned their heads to look through the bars of the stair rail, where they saw Brother Small pass quickly through the hallway beneath them, his keys rattling the entire way. He was gone almost as quickly as he had arrived. As the door swung shut, the two of them breathed a sigh of relief. Chad let of go of Tracey's head and the two of them pulled their faces apart. Chad was smiling, "That was a close . . ." he began to say, but Tracey interrupted.

"Let's get out of here. I do not want to get caught kissing you in school, especially not by Brother Small. My parents love Brother Small. Come on, let's get out of here." She reached for her bag and stood up. Chad just leaned back against the wall.

"I'm not going anywhere. He's not going to come back through here. It's after 4:15; nobody is around. Sit down, I promise nothing will happen."

"Chad," Tracey pleaded while sitting down uneasily. In a moment they were kissing again. A hundred feet away Brother Small opened the door to the O'Shaughnessy room and inspected the window. He had been worried that he might have to order a new window. But, upon inspecting it, he knew he would simply need to replace the hinge, a simple job, and he had plenty of hinges in his basement workshop. He shut off the lights, locked the door and headed back towards the Jesuit residence. Tracey and Chad were once again kissing ardently. They had situated themselves precariously on the landing so that one of each of their legs hung down over the top two steps on the flight of stairs.

When Brother Small opened the door, Tracey immediately pulled her leg back up onto the landing. Brother Small noticed the movement out of the corner of his eye. He took a few steps back and peered up into the darkness of the stairwell. He saw Tracey and Chad looking back at him out of the corners of their eyes. Chad once again had his hands on Tracey's face.

"Come on down from there," Brother Small called as sternly as he could. "This is no tunnel of love in here." Tracey grabbed her backpack and Chad pulled on his jacket. Brother Small stood on the landing below them and watched as the girl hesitated at the top of the stairs. "Come on, you've got to come down from up there." Tracey began to cry as she came down the steps. Brother Small was taken aback by the tears. As soon as she got to the bottom of the stairs Tracey began to apologize. Chad said nothing; he slid past Brother Small and down the stairs to the basement. "Brother Small, I'm so sorry. I knew we weren't supposed to be up there. We weren't really doing anything . . ."

"It's okay. It's okay; it's nothing to get too worked up about. Just don't do it again. You know you shouldn't behave like that in school. You have to respect this place and you have to respect yourself. Right? But don't make yourself crazy worrying about it. I won't hold it against you, okay?" He extended his hand; she shook it.

"Thank you."

"You're welcome."

Once Brother Small finally makes it back to his room, he takes a quick shower and changes into more comfortable clothes. After the shower, he sits in the only chair in his room, alone, and says his Rosary.

After fifteen or twenty minutes with the Rosary, Brother Small usually does a half-hour spiritual reading. Sometimes he reads and reflects on St. Ignatius' *Spiritual Exercises*. Sometimes he works on the book *Cloud of Unknowing*, which he used earlier today as a point in his morning prayer. Today, though, he will read from one of his favorites, a book called *Daily Readings with St. Teresa of Avila*. He normally picks a book he thinks will help facilitate deep reflection and then reads from it until he is particularly moved by a word or sentence. When this happens, he sets the book down and reflects on whatever idea or phrase has moved him.

Today he picks up the book and opens by chance to page 41, where the following reading titled "Look At Him" is printed.

> I am not asking you to make many reflections, to produce grand
>
> and subtle considerations with your intellect, or to feel deep devotion: I only ask you to look at Him.
>
> Who can prevent your turning the eyes of your soul (but for an instant, if you can do no more) on our Lord? You are able to look on many ugly things: then can you not gaze upon the fairest sight imaginable? Your bridegroom never takes His eyes off you!
>
> He has borne with many offences and much unworthiness in you, yet these have not sufficed to make him turn

away: is it much to ask that you should sometimes shift your
gaze from earthly things to fix it on Him?
You will find that he suits himself to whatever mood you
are in. He longs so keenly for our glance that he will neglect
no means to win it. (St. Teresa of Avila, pg.41)

"He longs so keenly for our glance," Brother Small repeats the
words to himself as he closes the book. Then he closes his eyes and
folds his hands in his lap. He sits there pondering the significance of
these words and their application in his life for nearly ten minutes. It
is just past five o'clock when he reopens his eyes.

"There are so many saints out there, why do you so look up to St.
Teresa of Avila?"

"For a lot of reasons, but here's a good story about why I am so
drawn to her life. Just yesterday, I was reading a book about Edith
Stein. She was a Jewish girl who lived in Germany. She was very intelligent and eventually became a professor of philosophy. In her studies, she came across the readings of St. Teresa, and she began to really
study them. After she had read St. Teresa's life, she said 'THAT IS
LIVING. THAT IS IT!' Eventually she converted and joined a
Carmelite Order. It was a very contemplative order. She fled Germany
during the holocaust, but the Nazis found her in Holland, and she
was killed in a concentration camp. She was an amazing woman; they
made her a saint. But, she also recognized that St. Teresa's life was
equally amazing, and she was right, St. Teresa just seemed to know
how to live."

"But what is it about St. Teresa that really inspires you?"

"Well, she was a marvelous writer and very down to earth. Her
writings are so good because her theology makes sense. Her views are
simple and she explains them so well. Loving God should not be a
hard concept to understand. It is a central concept with her, and she
approaches it simply. Sometimes certain ideas can be lost in theology.
Theology shouldn't be complicated, it should help people know God
and love God, and hers does. She is simple, yet she is so intelligent,

and beyond that, she is so loving. And I think that's why I like her so much, because she is so loving."

After his spiritual reading, Brother Small heads back down to the second floor of the Jesuit residence to his studio. He arrives at about 5:10 and he now has nearly forty-five minutes to work on finishing the painting Lynne Ryan will receive tonight as a gift for her forty-eighth birthday. In the next half-hour, he must begin to put his two people and rowboat into context. He has a rough sketch of the beach, water and the sky on the canvas, but there is still a good deal of work to be done.

A painting looks strange when it is not complete. In this painting, the two people are sitting and leaning up against the boat. There is sand around their feet and around the boat. The sand also stretches out behind them and begins to rise into the dunes, but it stops there. Beyond that point there is just white canvas. There are a few rough sketch marks on the painting indicating that the dunes will rise to fill that space. The rough lines also seem to indicate that the beach will stretch away from the two people until it runs out of sight in the distance at the point where it meets the water.

Right now, half of the canvas is still white; the beach disintegrates into nothing and the sky does not exist. The two people are staring at nothing; there is nowhere to go, nothing to live for. But, in a couple hours, the painting will be complete. It will be whole and it will make sense. It will be an accurate representation of the world, of a real scene and real people. During this afternoon session, Brother Small will complete the beach, which comprises much of the canvas space, and then try to begin finishing the sand dunes. He picks through the various piles of paint tubes spread around his studio until he finds the tan one he had used to begin the beach.

He opens the tube and squirts a generous amount of paint onto the palette. The palette is a mess of colors: some are original, and some others are mixtures of three or four different colors. He finds a clear spot for the tan and he works his brush into the paint, spreading it out, getting a feel for it. Then he sets to work on the canvas. He begins the beach at the spot where the sand will ultimately meet the water. He works backwards, quickly moving the sand on the beach towards the feet of the man and woman. Now he has a thick strip of sand running along the water as well as a mass of sand painted around and under his two subjects.

Soon he begins the brushstrokes that connect the strip with the sand, and slowly the beach takes shape. The seemingly abstract tan shapes come together to create a convincing beach. The picture works; it makes sense.

By 5:45 Brother Small has painted the entire beach as well as the first few waves rolling up against the beach. The man and woman are now on a complete beach watching the water slowly rise towards them and staring off into a sky of white canvas. Unfortunately he must stop there or he will miss dinner. Before dinner, he must swing by his workshop and pick up the frame he built earlier for Mrs. Ryan's painting. After dinner, he will return to his studio to try and finish what remains of the painting.

As Brother Small makes his way back towards his shop, he passes Ted Larkin, the coordinator of the Boys Hope Girls Hope Program, who has his back towards Brother Small as he talks quietly to a student. When Brother Small reaches Ted, he pats him gently on the back and says, "Working late tonight, huh, Ted?" Then he smiles at the student, a young woman with short chestnut hair, light brown skin and dark green eyes, and quietly says, "Hi there." The student nods slightly, and smiles shyly, as Brother Small continues down the hall. But Mr. Larkin calls to him quickly, "Brother Small, if you've got a minute, I'd like to introduce you to one of our scholars."

"I've always got a minute," Brother Small replies, turning quickly and walking back to them.

"This is Melanie Selva; she's a junior this year. Melanie, this is Brother Small. He's the guy to see if you need anything around here. He's a carpenter and a heck of a painter, too."

They shake hands. Melanie's hand is small and thin; it feels like it is almost all bone. Brother Small's expansive hand engulfs hers, but her grip is solid. They both speak at the same time. Brother Small says, "It's great to meet you." Melanie adds softly, "Nice to meet you." Brother Small pauses briefly and then continues talking, "Well, I'll let you all get back to your business." He turns and walks away.

Since she moved into Girls Hope, Melanie has had a chance to get involved at school, and to be a kid again. She joined the women's soccer team in the spring of her freshman year and scored three goals. She also sang in the fall musical, *Oklahoma*, at the beginning of her sophomore year.

Her grandmother presently lives in a nursing home in Wilmette, halfway between Girls Hope and Loyola. Melanie visits her every Saturday and on many Sundays. When she can, she also stops by to say hello during the week.

She has continued to do well in school. She's had her feet planted firmly on the first honor roll since she arrived at Loyola. For the first time in years, she has a group of friends with whom she spends much of her time both in and out of school.

One of her closest friends, Fletcher Purville, who is also a junior at Loyola and a resident at one of the Boys Hope homes, sits on the floor inside the office waiting for Mr. Larkin and Melanie to finish their conversation.

Fletcher and Melanie developed their friendship in Mr. Gier's geometry class, and on the late van rides home after practices for football and *Oklahoma* last fall. Fletcher's story is not totally unlike Melanie's. He hasn't seen either of his parents since he was three years old. His aunt raised him on the west side of Chicago, but he attended a grade school in Rogers Park, taking over an hour's worth of bus rides to get to school each day.

In April of his eighth-grade year, he had absolutely no idea what he would be doing the following year. His financial situation was uncertain and he didn't know if he'd be able to attend a private high school. But he knew he didn't want to go to the public school. So, he didn't do anything. He just spent his time shooting baskets after school, procrastinating and ignoring his future. A friend of his aunt's recognized his incredible potential as a student and referred him to the Boys Hope Girls Hope program. He got into the game late, but managed to plow through a frenzied battery of tests and entrance exams. He was accepted into the program.

Ted and Melanie make their way back into the office. Ted says nothing to Melanie or Fletcher about the financial contribution Brother Small makes to Loyola and the Boys Hope Girls Hope Program. They may never know. Brother Small certainly will never, ever say anything to them.

In fact, as he continues towards his shop, he doesn't even think about the fact that he is in part responsible for Melanie's opportunity to be at Loyola, or her opportunity to have a new home.

6

To labor and never ask for reward

We make a living by what we get,
but we make a life by what we give.

-Winston Churchill

It is dark in his workshop. The only light trickles through the filmy basement windows from the parking lot behind the school. Brother Small fumbles through his frames in the darkness until he finds Mr. Ryan's.

Then he closes the door and retraces his steps, with frame in hand. He sees another student just as he turns the last corner in the basement corridor. The student, clad in soccer shorts and shin guards, glances down the hall as Brother Small turns the corner. "Hi there," Brother Small says. "Hi," the student replies timidly, turning his face back towards his open locker.

Brother Small continues on, unaware of whom he has just passed. The student, Patrick Martin, fills his backpack with heavy textbooks, and brushes his long sweaty hair out of his face. He has never met Brother Small, and he is totally oblivious to the fact that the man who has made it possible for him and a number of other students to be at Loyola has just shuffled past him with a smile and a kind word.

Patrick Martin's life has been a difficult one. He has been bounced around a lot in the last couple years. He is presently living at Mike McDermott's house, and that is the third family he has lived with since he has been at Loyola.

Five years ago, in the middle of his seventh grade year, he decided he wanted to go to Loyola. He and his mother lived in Park Ridge and belonged to the Mary Seat of Wisdom parish. His father had left them just after Patrick's second birthday. They had heard from him only on rare occasions since his departure.

Patrick's mom did her best to raise him, but it was hard for her, financially and emotionally. She started working full time to support herself and Patrick. Her dedication to and love for her son kept her going, but they could not answer the questions about why her husband had left her totally alone.

She couldn't figure it out. Had she been a bad wife? Did her husband, also named Patrick, decide he just didn't want children? Was there another woman? It could have been anything really, but none of the possible scenarios made her feel better. At times she got very depressed, and it was difficult for her to motivate herself to continue working and, sometimes, living. During these down periods, she got sick and spent most of her free time in bed. She didn't really notice what was going on in Patrick's life, and he reacted by being mean to her, which only made the situation worse.

In the midst of one of these periods, Patrick came to her as she lay in bed half-asleep watching TV.

"Mom, you awake?" he asked trying not to wake her if she was asleep.

"Yeah, I'm up. What do you want?" she asked quietly without even opening her eyes.

"Um, well, this guy came to school today from Loyola, and he handed out some stuff about their school, and I kind of want to go there."

"Yeah? Well, what did the guy say?"

"He talked a lot about the school, and then a little bit about how expensive it was. Do we have enough money for me to go there?"

"Why don't we talk about it tomorrow, okay pal? My head hurts right now."

"Okay."

They didn't talk about it for a long time, not until November of Patrick's eighth grade year. It was almost a year later when he asked his mom to take him to the Loyola Academy Open House.

She did, and the two of them got a tour of the school from a junior on the soccer team. Patrick fell in love with the school. It was the first thing in his life he felt he really had to have. When they got into the car that night, Patrick's mom told him that she didn't think they would have enough money to send him there

"But, I guess there wouldn't be any harm in you taking the entrance exam," she added reluctantly.

So Patrick took the test six weeks later, on the first Saturday in January. His mom wasn't feeling well. So, he got himself out of bed and had a bowl of cereal. He found a ride with one of his classmates Tommy Lee, whose mom was driving to and from Loyola.

He took the test, and he walked out feeling like he had aced it. He could not have been happier, and he couldn't help but think that his mom was working on a way to pay for him to go to Loyola. He felt like he had gotten into the school, and now he had sort of convinced himself that he would be able to go there, with his mom's help, of course. After the test, he waited in front of the school for his ride. On the way home, he just stared out the window and daydreamed about playing soccer and making new friends at Loyola.

Before he knew it, Mrs. Lee was turning her big truck onto his street. As they rounded the final corner, Mrs. Lee slowed the car while she surveyed the scene at the end of the block. There was a fire truck, an ambulance and two police cars parked in front of Patrick's small house. She pulled up to the curb at the end of his driveway, and he climbed out of the car, thanking Mrs. Lee and Tommy and then walking slowly towards his house. As Patrick made his way up the drive, he noticed that the garage door was open and the red lights from the ambulance kept flashing on the back wall of the garage, where he and his mom hung their collection of plastic sleds. Most of the activity seemed to be centered there. Two policemen were writing things down, and the two paramedics were reaching into his mom's car. As Patrick continued up the drive, one of the policemen noticed him and hurried towards him. "Are you Patrick?" he asked him in an overtly hushed and somber voice.

"Yeah, I'm Patrick, and I live here. What's going on?"

"Why don't you come over here by the door and sit down for a minute." The two of them walked over and sat on the cracked concrete stoop in front of Patrick's front door.

"Patrick," the policeman began to say, and then he sighed, gathered himself and looked at Patrick again. "I have some bad news. I don't know how to say this. I wish I didn't have to tell you, but your mom took her own life this morning." He paused, giving Patrick an opportunity to speak, but he said nothing. "We're here to do anything we can for you; maybe we could begin by calling your dad." Patrick took a deep breath and just shook his head slowly, a lone tear running down his face. The policeman kept talking, but Patrick did not hear what he was saying.

He stared at the ground, and in a minute, he began to really cry. The policeman sat next to him, but Patrick didn't even notice him. His mind was filled with thoughts and questions about his mother. She was gone. Why did she do this to herself? What could have been so wrong that she would have killed herself? He did not understand.

He thought about his mother and her death. He didn't think about the fact that he was alone; his mom was an only child, too, so he had no aunts and uncles, and his grandparents were both dead. He didn't think about the fact that Loyola was now all but out of the question. He didn't even begin to worry about his own life. He just wondered what could have made his mom so terribly unhappy.

His mom had committed suicide. She had rolled down the passenger side window of her car, closed the garage door and started the engine. One of their neighbors had noticed the car running in the garage. This woman thought it was a strange situation. She checked back twenty minutes later. When she saw the car was still there she called the police.

Patrick had come home about forty-five minutes later. One of the neighbors his mom had been close to came and took him in. He went to the wake and the funeral with that family. After the funeral, the priest put his arm around Patrick and offered to help in any way. He said Patrick could come and talk to him and he would do anything in his power to make this easier for Patrick. He even offered to let Patrick live at the church, but Patrick declined. He had an offer from one of the neighbors and he thought he'd stay there.

A few weeks later, the scores from Patrick's entrance exam arrived at his house. He had passed, but he had not only passed, he'd done so with flying colors: his scores had been in the top ten percent of everyone who had taken the test. Soon thereafter he went to see the priest. They talked for a long time about Patrick's life now and how he felt about it. Towards the end of their conversation, Patrick said, "Father, I really want to go to Loyola. Do you know how I can find out if there is money somewhere I can use to do that?"

The priest, Father Maggio, told Patrick he would try to help him figure it out. He kept his word and worked diligently on this for Patrick. But, the results were not encouraging. There was very little money left. His mom had not had life insurance since his dad left. She was way overdue on the house and car payments. Father Maggio did not immediately tell Patrick that there was no money. Rather he tried to raise enough money through people in the parish to pay Patrick's tuition at Loyola. This idea did not work either. While the parishioners were generous, they did not give enough to get Patrick through even his first year at Loyola. So, Fr. Maggio called the school. He introduced himself and then began to explain why he was calling.

"There is a boy in my Parish who would like to go to your high school, but because of a recent family tragedy he does not have enough money to attend the school."

"Well, he and his parents can come into the school and speak with someone in the financial aid office."

"He doesn't have parents, ma'am. His mother just recently died and his father left when he was just a young child."

"Well, I guess you should come in with him then."

That settled it. Fr. Maggio called Patrick and told him that they had a date to go to Loyola in a week and that they would meet with the financial aid director. The meeting went well. Loyola would pay almost the entire tuition. The rest could be covered by the donations from the parishioners.

Patrick finally had his dream. He still did not have a permanent home or the family stability around which he could build a normal life. But, he did have a chance to attend Loyola.

He has since lived with three different families in his two and a half years of high school, but this has not hindered his progress. He has succeeded athletically and academically. He is part of the honors program and has made the soccer team in each of his first three years, this year starting for the varsity team as a junior. He has already heard from a couple of college soccer coaches. If he does not get a scholarship to play soccer, he may be able to get an academic scholarship.

Patrick is part of the 12% of Loyola's student population who receives financial aid from the school. The money, which enables these 240 or so students to attend Loyola, comes from a number of sources. Many of the alumni donate; and some companies and foundations also make sizable donations. Loyola's most generous benefactors are displayed on a plaque in the foyer of the school. The following inscription is engraved on the plaque, "Loyola honors the special generosity of the following corporations and foundations, alumni and friends. Their commitment at the highest level to the ministry of Jesuit Education at the Academy merits the distinction of being named Lifetime Founders."

The plaque commemorates those who have made lifetime contributions totaling over $100,000. Brother James E. Small's name has been on the plaque for quite a few years: he can't remember how many exactly. Nice contribution from a guy who has not cashed a paycheck since 1952.

At six o'clock every night, before they have dinner together, the Jesuits gather in their dining room for a community prayer. These ten Jesuits who assemble loudly in the dimly lit dining room atop Loyola Academy are bonded to one another by their lives of service and spirituality. Their lives of service are self-explanatory. Their lives of spirituality can be a little more difficult to comprehend. For these ten men, living in and of the spirit is a life-defining task. But being spiritual, or developing a working spirituality is not an easy thing to do. Being spiritual is not even an easy thing to understand. According to Richard McBrien, a preeminent Catholic theologian "To live according to the spirit is to enjoy "life and peace." But how can one achieve this peace and happiness? What does it mean to live according to the spirit? McBrien explains,

> To be spiritual means to know, and to live according to that knowledge, that there is more to life than meets the eye. To be "spiritual" means, beyond that, to know, and to live according to the knowledge, that God is present to us in grace as the principle of personal, interpersonal, social and even cosmic transformation. To be "open to the spirit" is to accept explicitly who we are and who we are called always to become and to direct our lives accordingly. (McBrien, 1,057)

Spirituality, according to McBrien, is a function of knowledge, but above and beyond that, it is a way to be. We are all human beings, but how do we choose to be? How do we choose to live? McBrien suggests that spirituality is an understanding of God's presence, but it is also the act of living out that understanding of God. Thus, finding a spirituality, or being spiritual, is in many ways a life-defining task.

Jesuit spirituality relies heavily on prayer. The Jesuits use prayer time as an opportunity to gather knowledge or understanding about God. But, prayer is far from the main function of the Jesuits. The Jesuits are not a cloistered order; they do not live within the closed walls of a monastery. Their mission is with people, and their spirituality focuses on trying to imitate Christ in every aspect of their daily lives and putting their love into action. Jesuit spirituality involves looking for God in all things, and living Ad Majorem Dei Gloria, for the greater glory of God.

It seems like a sensible, maybe even a simple life. Know God, then imitate God; follow in his footsteps; do his will. But, is a Jesuit's life really that simple? No, not at all. While they strive to live lofty lives of ideals, the Jesuits are human beings riddled with faults just like the rest of us. But still, Brother Small and his Jesuit counterparts have chosen to try to dedicate their lives to God. How? Why? It's an amazing choice, and an amazing life, but it is far from simple. I had an opportunity to learn that firsthand when I was a senior at Loyola and I got the following letter in my homeroom mail.

> Dear George,
> Your name has been mentioned as a possible candidate for the Jesuits. We would like to talk to you about this possibility. We understand that you may not have considered the Jesuits as part of your future. Either way we would like to share with you some of our experiences and insights on religious life. So, please join us in two weeks on Saturday, the sixteenth of October at 5:00 PM in the Jesuit residence for an informal pizza dinner.
> Thank you.
> Sincerely,
> Loyola's Jesuits

I read through the letter and promptly crumpled it up. I had never thought about being a priest, and I was actually embarrassed to have received the letter. "Why in the world would they choose me?" I thought to myself as I fingered the ball of paper in my pocket. A few minutes later, I decided to skip the dinner and threw the letter in the garbage.

Later in the week, I ran into Father Ytsen, one of the few Jesuit teachers at Loyola. I had taken Father Ytsen's British Literature class junior year. He asked me if I would be coming to the dinner.

"No, it's just that, well, I just don't think I'm cut out for the priesthood."

"Nobody said you were, and if you come to dinner, we won't make you sign anything. I'm guessing you've never really thought about it and you are just giving me a cop-out answer, right?" I nodded in agreement.

"So, come to dinner. We'll talk and, if you think we're crazy, that's fine. By then you'll at least know what we're all about, and you'll have a little bit of knowledge on the subject. What do you say?"

"Well, I'll think about it, what do I have to lose?"

"Except," I thought to myself, "a normal life, with a wife and kids and everything else in the world."

"Good, we'll see you Saturday."

So on the following Saturday I attended the meeting, somewhat reluctantly. To be honest, I entered the room with no intention of becoming a Jesuit, and when I left I still did not plan on being a priest, but I did unknowingly stumble into one of the most profound learning experiences of my life.

Before the meeting I had never really understood that there were normal people behind the religious garments. When I heard the word "priest" I thought of old men, gray and callous, distant, robed, standing behind altars. I always saw them alone, and I understood them to be fundamentally different than myself. I was very wrong in most of my assumptions.

The four Jesuits present at the meeting had begun by saying that the purpose of the gathering was for the five of us students to learn something about their lives. "So, ask us anything. You can ask us any question about our lives. We never had an opportunity to sit down with anyone like this when we were thinking about joining the Jesuits, and we think it would have been useful for us. So, go ahead."

There were five students. We asked all kinds of questions; we talked for nearly three hours. Right off the bat one of the other guys said, "Don't you guys have to take vows of poverty and chastity?"

"Yes," Fr. Ytsen answered, "we take a number of vows when we are ordained, two of which are chastity and poverty."

"Well, I don't mean to be rude," the student said, "but this doesn't really look like poverty to me," he said as he waved his hand around the room towards the fireplace, the wood floors, the expansive windows, and the comfortable furniture.

"No, this is not poverty at all. We live very comfortable lives here. The residence is beautiful, and we eat three meals a day. The vow of poverty means that we cannot become tied to any of this." The student looked confused, and Fr. Ytsen leaned forward in his seat as he continued to explain.

"When I say we cannot be tied to any of this, it simply means we have to be ready to leave it. It does not mean we cannot enjoy it. One thing you have to understand is that we don't own this stuff, the residence, the cars, the food; it belongs to the school, or the order, not to us as individuals, but we are provided for. However, tonight I could get a phone call, and the Jesuit superior could be on the other end of the line, and he could tell me 'Bob, pack your bags, tomorrow morning you are going to Malaysia.' Just like that I could be gone. I could probably take one bag, and I wouldn't have room for much more than the essentials. This would stay, and so would these." As he said this he grabbed the Polo monogram on his shirt, and tapped the tops of his leather dress shoes. "The vow of poverty means that we as Jesuits cannot become attached to these worldly items; we have to be prepared and willing to leave them behind." He paused for a moment, "And I guess the vow of chastity is pretty much self-explanatory."

"Its definition is self-explanatory," I said, "but I'm not sure I understand how you deal with it, you know, emotionally or physically."

"What do you mean by that?" Fr. Ytsen inquired.

"Well, I understand what it is, but I don't know if I understand why it's necessary, or how you do it. First of all, what is the problem with you guys being married? Second, do you feel lonely without another person in your life, another person who you can, well, I guess be sexually intimate with, or someone who you can have kids with?"

"A lot of people ask about the purpose of celibacy, or how necessary it is in this day and age. Suffice it to say, I believe in it. All of us here have two jobs. I am a teacher, so is Dr. Godleski, Brother Small is a carpenter; Father Humbert is the alumni director. But beyond that we all have chosen to dedicate our lives to God. As a result, knowing God is in a sense a job for us, albeit a job we cherish and love. As such, it requires a very serious commitment. It is not easy to see God, or to know God in our daily lives, and if we cannot see God, we cannot follow God. So, we have to work at it; just as we work at our jobs, we work at this, mostly through prayer. It's a lot of work, though. It can take a couple of hours a day."

"Yeah, but, you can still see God and follow God if you're married, right?"

"In a sense you're right, I am no different than my dad or your dad in terms of the ability to find God. But I am different in the amount of time I have that I can dedicate to that task. If I had a family, either my family or my relationship with God would receive less attention than it deserves, and I have to take care of my relationship with God. It is a decision I made a long time ago, and one I have never regretted."

"Okay, but why, why did you make that decision?" I inquired.

"Knowing God, and seeing God makes me see everything more clearly. And seeing God makes me alive, not alive in the sense of physical functions but alive. I mean really alive, vibrant, rich and true. God makes my life complete."

"I can understand that," I replied. "I may not have had similar experiences, but I think I understand what you are saying. However, I am still curious if you feel you are missing part of life. I guess what I am asking you is don't you ever want a family, a wife, kids . . ?"

"Every day. Not a day goes by when I don't dream that I could hold a baby, not to baptize it, but to have it be mine, my own flesh and blood, part of me, part of all of me. I would love to have a child, and I think married life would be fantastic, but becoming a priest was something I had to do, and I have no complaints."

I learned so much in those three hours that I spent with the Jesuits. I learned that the Jesuits are people just like me. I think this fact is often overlooked or forgotten. I know I didn't realize it before the meeting. Jesuits are normal people too. Their status as religious figures does not change the fact that they live, love and die just like the rest of us.

Sometimes it is easier to assume that they are different. A lot of people make the assumption that most priests and brothers must be gay. How else could they choose to live without women? Another common misconception is that none of them could attract women, and a religious life was the only thing left.

Both of these statements are inaccurate. In fact, two of the four Jesuits in the meeting I attended were engaged to be married when they made the decision to become Jesuits.

The lives of these Jesuits are not always easy. The process of gathering knowledge and translating it into a living mission is a difficult one. Becoming a Jesuit means saying no to wealth, marriage, sexual intimacy and family, the things that define and lend meaning to many people's lives.

However, it means saying yes to God, a life in and of God. But this kind of life is not always easy; it requires lots of work. It is a job that depends on a strong spirituality.

So at 6:00 PM every night, the Jesuits gather and pray as a community so that they may help each other to be more spiritual. Each night, they share a community prayer. Each night, one of the ten Jesuits in the community leads the prayer which can last anywhere from thirty seconds to fifteen minutes.

Tonight it is Brother Small's turn. Everyone sits down together at the two spacious tables in the Jesuit residence, and he opens the prayer book and begins to read from a prayer called "To Love and Serve All Things," written by St. Ignatius.

"God is Love, and anyone who lives in love, lives in God."

They all reply, "God's love for us was revealed when he sent his only son into the world."

Brother Small continues, "This is love, not our love for God, but God's love when he sent his son."

They all respond, "Since God loved us so much, we too ought to love one another."

Brother Small continues, "If you close your heart to the brother you see, how can you claim to love God who you do not see?"

They reply, "And our love is not to be just words and talk but true love, showing itself in action and deeds."

The prayer lasts for about four more minutes.

Afterwards Brother Small asks, "Are there any special intentions tonight?" A couple of the Jesuits speak up, "For the girls on Kairos." The rest of them nod their heads and reply, "Lord hear our prayer."

"For Fr. Humbert, that he may be restored to health." Fr. Bob Humbert SJ, one of the older Jesuits at Loyola, who has served the school loyally for decades, has recently fallen ill. Again they say in unison, "Lord hear our prayer."

"For all of the sick men up at Colombiere." It is the retirement home and infirmary for all of the elderly and ill Jesuits in the Midwest. "Lord hear our prayer."

"For Ted, that his retreat is a good one." Fr. Theodore Munz SJ is the president of the school, and he is making his required annual eight-day retreat this week.

These retreats are one of the most fundamental elements of Jesuit spirituality. In his time as a Jesuit, Brother Small has been on two thirty-day retreats, and dozens of eight-day retreats. This year he will make his eight-day retreat with close friend Brother Haas. For years Brother Small and Brother Haas made their retreats with Fr. John Beall, a longtime Jesuit who worked as the dean and chaplain at Loyola for thirty years before being transferred to a Catholic high school in Lexington Kentucky. Father Beall unfortunately passed away on May 22, 1999.

In a few months, Brother Small and Brother Haas will make only their second retreat without him. They will however return to the same vacation home in northern Wisconsin, donated by friends, where they have been going for the past decade.

"Is a retreat a joyous time or a somber time?"

"Well, both. Retreats are a very serious time, but I look forward to them so much each year, much more so than any vacation I could ever take. But a retreat is not a vacation. The first three days are tough. We don't realize how wound up we become in our world, how much tension there is in our physical bodies and our minds and our spirituality. It's hard to forget about those things, but on my retreats I can become peaceful. I don't think about my job or my worries, and I am able to put myself in a new frame of mind. A retreat is an exciting and joyous time because it helps me get back on track; it helps me to live the life I want to live."

Any Jesuit retreat based on the spiritual exercises, whether it be eight days or thirty, begins with the first principle. This principle, which involves the retreatant attempting to become aware of God's call at the time of the retreat, is a literal and figurative foundation for the rest of the retreat. In this initial block of time, the retreatant attempts to simply touch base with God, to once again focus on listening to God, and thereby prepare himself for the remainder of the retreat.

The next section of one of Brother Small's retreats is filled with meditations on sin. In this segment, Brother Small says he reflects on the sin of angels, the sin of Adam and Eve and the sin of man.

"What is sin? What does it mean to sin?"

"I think people today forget about the idea of sin a lot," he says, "but look at Adam and Eve, that one sin alone has brought us suffering, immorality and death." He continues to explain this section of the retreat and then concludes by saying, "When I reflect on sin, I realize I am lucky, and that God loves me, because I realize that I have not been punished for all of my sins."

In the second segment of a typical eight-day Jesuit retreat, the prayers and meditations are focused on the life of Christ on earth. Brother Small explains this part of the retreat in terms of one particular meditation, the meditation on the Kingdom of God. "God wants everybody to be under his banner, he wants us all to follow him," he explains matter-of-factly, "to fight for what is right and to help bring people to heaven. Now I can say that, sure, it's easy to say. But how do I do it? Well, I say, okay, I need a plan. I must find somebody whose life I can emulate." As he says this, it is clear that he has thought about it and that he is excited about it. He is speaking faster than he normally does, gesturing enthusiastically with his hands. "Well, I am going to pick Christ to emulate, but in order to do that I need to know how he lived and what he did. I need to know everything he did. I must understand his life and his love. I need to study him. I need to know the New Testament, you see, because everything he did was for a purpose, to show me the way. Every time he helped somebody, I should try to do the same."

This section of the retreat is geared towards preparing for the future. It is a way to get to know Christ better and, therefore, become better prepared to follow him. During this time on the retreat, Brother Small tries to answer the following questions:

"What does it take for me to follow Christ?

What does it mean for me to love my neighbor as I love myself?

What would Christ do if faced with the same situation facing me?

How can I fashion my life after Christ's life?"

"Does it take courage to follow Christ in this world that tends not to focus on the same things Christ focused on or lived for or, more importantly, died for?"

"Oh yes, it does, it takes a great deal of courage. It's so easy to go along with the crowd in whatever we are doing. It is safer that way, and that's what we do a lot of the time because we don't want to stand out, because we don't want to look like a holier-than-thou. It does take courage to follow Christ, and it can be difficult. Some people don't like that type of life. Living that way means that you'll probably lose some of your friends."

The third portion of Brother Small's retreat involves meditating on the passion of Jesus, the days leading up to his death and the crucifixion itself. The fourth and final segment of the retreat focuses on Jesus' resurrection.

The long retreats and some of the shorter Jesuit retreats also include another very important reflection, which does not fit neatly into any of the other four sections. This day is spent on the contemplation to obtain divine love. This portion of the retreat is dedicated to studying all of the ways in which God loves us. Again Brother Small explains, "The contemplation to obtain divine love, well in a long retreat, there's usually one day you spend on that meditation, one whole day. What you do is make a list of all the gifts you have received.

You've received the gift of life; you're here; God brought you on this earth. You've got a soul. You've got your health, you can walk, you can get out of bed in the morning, you can see. You've got wonderful family. You've got an education. You have a place to live. And you have always been fed well. God has made sure you have always had enough to eat, and entertainment, and on, and on, and on.

The list gets bigger and bigger of all the things he's done for you. Everyone always asks 'what has he done for **me**?' But just analyze the situation and you realize you're not suffering any pain right now. You're in good health, you're happy, and you're physically able to do almost anything you want. These things are all gifts from God.

The more you analyze a thing, the more you realize God is right there in that thing. But, many people don't stop and think; they just get on the bus and go to work so that they can support their families."

"What is the most important thing a retreat does?"

"A retreat changes your whole outlook on life. After a year's time, you wear down and can't see the port you're heading for. Things get blurry, we lose sight of what is important, and we lose sight of our priorities. Retreats help to bring everything back into perspective. Every time I go on a retreat, I come back renewed...that's really what it is: a renewal of spirit . . . and it energizes me about my life and my work."

"Imagine you meet the 50-year-old mother of a Loyola student, who has never been on a retreat. What would you tell her about a retreat? Why should she go?"

"I'd tell her a retreat will not only benefit you, but it will change your life. But there is only one way to find out, you must take my word for it and do it, and you'll find out it will definitely change your life for the better. I guarantee that you will come back a different person and a better person."

Once the Jesuits in Loyola's community have prayed for all of their special intentions and concluded their evening prayer, they begin their meal. Tonight they are having pot roast, mashed potatoes, gravy, a salad and a loaf of fresh bread.

7

Save that of knowing that I do your will.

A Christian is a line through which
Jesus Christ thinks . . . a heart through
which Jesus Christ loves, a voice
through which Jesus Christ speaks
. . . and a hand through which
Jesus Christ heals.
                                        -G. Mueller

After dinner, Brother Small doesn't sit and read the newspaper or lounge in front of the TV. Instead, he heads down to his studio for a long painting session, his favorite way to wind down at the end of the day. He retires to the small stuffy room on the second floor where he once again allows his creative instincts to reign supreme, this time for an hour and a half. Tonight will not be as relaxing as some evenings because at eight o'clock Brother Small is meeting Tim Ryan in the parking lot behind the Jesuit residence. By then he hopes to have Mrs. Ryan's painting done, with the rest of the sand, sky, water and the frame he built earlier in the day.

When Brother Small enters the room he flips on the radio to the sweet sound of a violin and piano working in harmony to create a beautiful melody that he would never even try to identify.

He reaches for his red women's glasses, places them on his face and situates himself behind the easel. He quickly sets to work on finishing Lynne Ryan's picture. He studies the original poster for a moment and then looks over the work he has finished so far on his canvas.

The first order of business is completing the dunes behind the beach. The beach presently stretches from the two subjects in front of the boat down to the water. But behind the boat, which rests in the center of the picture, the beach rises quickly into a series of hilly dunes. The music draws to a close, and the disc jockey says, *"After a few messages, we will have the evening news, and then we'll return to Chicago's best classical music."*

"Is your hair thinning?" the voice booms out of the radio into the quiet of Brother Small's sanctuary. *"I'm Brian Reichenberg with Kevis. There are drugs available that may restore your hair. With advances in science, the question is not does a product grow hair, but which product offers you the most benefits for your hair. Thousands of Kevis clients have enjoyed thicker, fuller, healthier-looking hair without the risk of side effects. Call 888-926-HAIR. That's 888-926-HAIR."*

"Are you concerned with your physical appearance?"

"No, not really. My spiritual well being is more important to me than my physical condition or appearance. When I was young and I was worried about the girls, I used to really care about how I looked. But, now what difference does it make? I guess now I could probably dress a little bit better and try to look a little bit nicer, but clothes mean nothing to me. Looks really don't mean anything anymore. Look at me, how could they? I don't like to look in the mirror or even look at pictures anymore. I'm old now; that's old age. But, I don't feel old. It's a big mystery; I always thought old people must feel old. But I don't. When I am with you, and when I am talking to you, I feel like I am your age. Pretty girls are still pretty. Our minds stay young. In some ways, I still feel like I am twenty-one years old. I want to do everything I can. I want to keep working like I did when I was twenty-one. But, pretty soon I'm afraid, I will begin to slow down."

"Are you afraid of the day you begin to slow down, or the day you die?"

"No, I'm not afraid of death. It's part of original sin, so I am concerned about death. But, if you look at the big picture, the closer you get to death, the happier you should be. Years ago I worked with a Jesuit with the last name Kemper. There were three Kemper brothers in the Society. Their sister was a nun; she was a superior for years in Japan. When she was close to death, they brought her back to the United States. 'Are you afraid of death?' they asked her. 'No I'm not afraid to die, I am just ashamed to die.' That's how I feel about death.

I'm not worried about the consequences, I just wish I could have done better in life."

Brother Small mixes a touch of white oil paint in with the tan he had been using for the sand. He works the two shades into an empty spot on his palette and creates a sandy beige that will work well in the dunes. He covers the brush with paint and begins to craft the dunes with quick vertical brush strokes as the next commercial begins.

"Is your career taking you where you want to go? Would better business knowledge and skills allow you to move ahead or even change direction? If so, we have a suggestion, test drive an MBA at the Lake Forest Graduate School of Management; come to one of our February open houses and become a graduate student for a night. Sit in on a class; meet members of our faculty, CEO's, CFO's and leaders of Chicago industry. Talk with our students who average 11 years in the business world. Experience the special chemistry between our teachers and students and see how different we are from other schools; take the guesswork out of one of the most important decisions of your life. See for yourself that people just like you have gone back for their MBA's and are succeeding at it, accelerating their careers like you can accelerate yours. Come to one of our February open houses at our campuses in Lake Forest, Schaumburg and Downtown Chicago. Call 1-800-737-4MBA, 1-800-737-4MBA."

"Do you feel like you missed out on a college education?"

"Oh, yeah, I definitely feel like I missed out on that, and if things would have worked out differently, I might have been able to go to college. High school education back then was probably the same as a college education is now. I would have liked to go, but I don't think education is the most important thing in the world either. I think there is a lot of vanity in education. So many people insist on going to college, but they never use anything they learned in their education. Is it really all that necessary? Do you need to pay $20,000 a year for school in order to bring welfare to yourself and to the other people around you? That's the big question, and sometimes I think we assume that we cannot do anything without a college education. But, that is not true; no matter who you are, you can do something to help yourself and, beyond that, to help other people."

"How do you define success?"

"When I am on my deathbed, and I look back on my life, I hope I will be able to say, 'I did the best I could.' If I can say that, then I think I will have been successful, no matter what I did. How will I feel when I am on my deathbed? It's a good thought exercise, especially when you are making important decisions about life, like your occupation. Are you doing something that satisfies you? Will it satisfy you when your life is over? You should feel as though you did the best you could, whether it was as a religious, or as a father or a mother. Did I keep the Commandments as well as I could? Did I love God as much as I could? Did I love my neighbor as myself? I think success is in how we live and not in our accomplishments or accumulations."

H e works around the back of the boat and begins to creep higher on the canvas as the dunes rise. He uses green paint to add a few patches of grass to the top of the dunes, as well as a big patch reaching down onto the beach in the distance behind the two people. The bottom two thirds of the picture are now complete. The boat sits in the center of the canvas, the man sitting next to it, and the woman leaning against it. They are presently looking off into the vast whiteness of the rest of the canvas. The beach stretches out before them, and the dunes rise up behind them; but the beach stretches towards nothing, and the dunes rise up to emptiness. It is just a couple minutes past seven o'clock when the inane commercials draw to a momentary close to make way for the evening news.

"Today high school administrators and security forces attended an all day workshop at the Williams Bay High School in southeastern Wisconsin. The subject? How to prepare for and react to school shootings. In the wake of the Littleton disaster, where thirteen people were gunned down by two students, schools across the country have taken action. 'We need to do something. There just isn't a standard

anymore, we can't take things for granted. Unfortunately, we must be prepared for the worst.' That was Rod Smith a principal from the nearby Delevan-Darien High School. He added that the workshop seemed to be a success and everyone present left with a better understanding of the dangers presented by school shooters.

Certain groups in corporate America are taking similar steps after Mark Barton killed nine people in two different Atlanta day trading offices. Three security companies are presently offering seminars on how businesses can protect themselves from the possibility of violent attacks in their offices. "Who knows what people will do anymore? You just can't be too careful," said Michael Toms, a mechanical contractor whose company recently completed one of the seminars.

In the suburbs, a pregnant woman was hit and killed by a car. The accident took place just after nine o'clock last night at the entrance to Flick Park in North Suburban Glenview. The twenty-year old driver fled but was quickly apprehended. He has admitted to driving under the influence of drugs and alcohol."

"Do you think something is wrong with our society? How can it be remedied?"

"Yes, something is definitely wrong. Just look at the news and you can see. I think the cause of the problem is very simple. We have taken God out of our lives. In order to make things better, we must teach religion and values, and morality, and the Ten Commandments at home and in the school. We need to have God in our lives whether it is at work, at home, in movies or even in TV.

There has been a breakdown in values, because God is not alive anymore for so many people. And when that happens the Commandments become meaningless. You can see how this works in our society, from the top on down. The President can't come close to keeping the Commandments."

"Is the world we live in essentially good or bad?"

"I think the world is essentially good. We do all suffer from original sin and fight against it constantly. There is certainly room for improvement; our world has so many problems. I guess all you can do is try to make improvements in small ways each day. If everybody did that, think how far we could get. Even with all of the problems, it is important to remember that life is a blessing, and for that reason it is good and beautiful, and will always be essentially good."

"What has been your impact on the world?"

"Well, I think my impact on the world has been very small, if I've had an impact at all. Most people don't know I exist, but that doesn't really matter as long as God knows me and knows I love Him, and as long as I love God. All of that is true, but still I feel that I have fallen way short of God's expectations for me, but I will just keep trying until the end."

"Do you feel like you can change the world?"

"Well, all I can say is that Christ said that we, his followers, will be able to do many more things and touch even more people than He Himself did. With modern communication, TV, newspapers, and movies, it is possible for us to do as much as Christ did and much more, at least in terms of the number of people we can reach. A lot more people have heard Bing Crosby's voice than ever heard Jesus' voice. Now, I am not comparing myself to Christ, don't get me wrong, but I do have a unique opportunity to love and serve more people than Jesus was ever able to do Himself."

In New Jersey a high school girl and her boyfriend were arrested at their homecoming dance after they were caught stuffing the body of their newborn infant into a dishwasher in the school cafeteria. The girl gave birth to the child in the bathroom at the school. Then she and the father took the infant into the cafeteria. They were discovered there locking the baby into one of the industrial sized dishwashers.

And now, financial news. It was a strong day in the American markets. Heavy trading drove prices higher as people continued to buy up blue chips and Internet stocks. Today's mini-rally was fueled by splits in some of the major tech stocks, namely Microsoft. McDonald's also announced a two-for-one split today and the stock was rewarded up three and five-eighths. The Dow finished up one hundred-thirty-

seven-points. The S&P finished up nineteen and the NASDAQ neared a new high, up fifty-five on the day to close at 4,192. The big question: how long will this incredible growth last? Andy Moorekash, an analyst from Goldman Sachs has an answer: "Right now, we're seeing incredible consumer confidence. The market has been so strong lately it has finally given people something to rely on and believe in. As long as everyone continues to believe this thing will keep going like this, it will, and everybody will continue to make money."

"A few words from our sponsors and we'll return to the music."

"Homeowners are you tired of empty promises from mortgage companies for rates under seven percent but when the time comes to close those rates disappear?

U.S. Mortgage and Acceptance Corporation was created to help homeowners whose credit proves they are only human. After all, the credit problems of yesterday shouldn't keep you from benefiting from today's low mortgage rates. Call USMAC now and turn those promises into real savings even if you've had a past bankruptcy or foreclosure.

If you're tired of those promised under seven percent rates that never seem to happen and you want to start saving money, consolidate some bills, or just get some extra cash, call USMAC your direct lending source at 1-800-840-C-A-S-H

Take advantage of today's low interest rates. Call USMAC an Illinois mortgage licensee and an equal opportunity lender at 1-800-840-CASH 1-800-840-C-A-S-H."

"You have never really focused on material things, why not? What are the advantages to living that way?"

"By living what people call a 'simple life,' I feel I've got more time to concentrate on why I am here in this life, and more time to concentrate on what I should be doing for God.

I haven't always felt this way. At different times in my life I focused on material things. For a long time I was hung up on cars. I had a Lincoln one time, before I joined the Jesuits. I liked cars; I liked everything everybody else liked: cars, good food, friends, and good drinks. I still like all these things. I enjoy good food and a good bed so that I can rest at night. But now I know that I don't need many things. I can survive without material things; not only that, I am happy with my life without these things. I'm not sure I realized that I could be happy before I ever tried to live without them."

"Do you think less of people who focus all their attention on things?"

"I try not to pass judgments on other people, so I guess I don't give it much thought one way or another. If a person has worked hard for what they have and they got their money legitimately, that's great. Let them enjoy life."

Brother Small quickly squeezes some blue into a small clear square on his palette. The sea should not take long at all. It covers a very small area on the canvas and he has already painted part of it. The water itself occupies just a small sliver of the painting and he quickly fills in this space with a crystalline mix of light blue and white paint. The light shade of blue, however, does not look convincing as seawater until he adds a series of white crests breaking softly onto the wet sand. Somehow the addition of these white streaks brings the sea to life. It goes from a flat blue triangle, to moving water. He adds more white to the water near the beach where the waves are rolling gently up onto the sand, as the next commercial begins with a score of marching band music. Brother Small taps his toes to the music, but does not seem to hear the words.

"What are you searching for? What would make you happy? A Wylie Coyote cookie jar? Well, there's this place; it's called E-BAY. That's E-B-A-Y.com. But hold on E-shoppers-this is no Internet version of any store you'll find anywhere else on earth. E-Bay is your marketplace for the truly amazing stuff. Hey, where else would you find an original set of Lincoln Logs, you know, the ones made out of wood? Or that Captain Picard as a Borg figure? E-Bay is the genuine article, an original, kind of like everything you'll find there. About a million cool things every day neatly organized into about a thousand separate categories. And once you find it, you decide what it's worth

because everything is sold auction style, so come for a visit,
www.ebay.com, the one and only. Oh, and happy hunting."

"What are you searching for?"

"To do God's will. I just want to find out what God wants and do it.
I try to do that day after day. I don't always succeed, but that is the
object of my life; that is the thing I am searching for. I think it should
be the object of everyone's life. Whether it is or not, I don't know, but
it should be."

He continues with the white paint. As the music begins again
he creates a series of clouds hanging over the horizon in the distance.
The clouds are bright white on the edges, but darker in the middle,
and they seem to be slowly rolling in towards the beach. Above the
clouds he returns to blue although now it is a much lighter shade of
blue. He has filled the canvas with a perfect afternoon sky. He sits
back and looks at his work, and then glances at his watch. It is now
seven forty-four. He will need five minutes to fit the picture into the
frame and get downstairs, which gives him ten to let it sit and dry.

At five minutes to eight, Brother Small carefully lifts the painting,
making sure not to touch the areas where the paint will still be wet.
He picks it up and fastens it into the frame. He will have to put the
backing on the frame later. From the front, the picture and the frame
both look perfect.

Four minutes after eight he is standing at the back door of the
Jesuit residence when Tim Ryan pulls up in a dark green Cadillac.

"Brother Small, how are you tonight?" he calls out as he walks
towards Brother Small.

"Very well, Tim, and yourself?"

"Can't complain." As he says this, he leans down and peeks at the
painting, which is presently leaning against the wall.

"Here it is," Brother Small announces as he picks it up and turns
it over. "Be careful though, it's still wet."

"Oh, wow, this looks great, a whole lot better than that poster." He
takes the picture out of Brother Small's hands and admires it. He

smiles broadly as he studies the intricacies of the painting. "She's gonna love this." He sets the picture down and reaches for his pocket, "What do I owe you, Brother?"

"Nothing, nothing," Brother Small replies. "It was a favor."

"Who should I make the check out to, you?"

"No, you really don't need to write a check," Brother Small counters. As he says this Mr. Ryan begins to write *Brother James Small* on the check. "No, no, if you're going to write one, please make it out to Loyola Academy or else to the Loyola Frame Shop."

"No problem." Mr. Ryan tears out the check with Brother Small's name on it and begins another. He makes this one thousand five hundred-dollar check out to Loyola. "Okay, Brother, now can I give you something?" he says as he prepares to begin another check.

"No sir, this goes to my shop and the school and we both are very thankful, but please, no more."

"Well, I can at least thank you. I really appreciate you working so hard to get this done. So will Lynne."

"It's a great picture; I enjoyed working on it," Brother Small says.

As he walks back up the steps to the Jesuit residence, he folds up Tim Ryan's check and tucks it into his shirt pocket. He uses the money he makes from his frame shop and his painting commissions to buy new painting and framing supplies. However, at the end of each year, Brother Small has accumulated somewhere between ten and fifteen thousand dollars. In addition, he has spent that much replenishing his supply of paint, canvas and molding for the frames he builds. He does not keep any of this left over cash. He has taken a vow of poverty. He hands it over to Loyola's Jesuit community, just like he hands over all of his forty-two thousand five hundred dollar carpenter's salary.

At the end of the year, the Jesuit community splits up all the extra money and gives it to various charities and schools, including Boys Hope Girls Hope, Cristo Rey Jesuit High School and Loyola Academy. Once in the hands of the schools, some of the money is used for financial aid and eventually makes its way to students like Patrick

Martin and Melanie Selva, who because of their families' circumstances would never have been able to attend a Jesuit high school without it.

The money Brother Small earns goes many places and does many things. He never knows where for sure, but he likes it that way. He makes a huge impact at the school, but he does it silently, almost anonymously. He's not concerned with where the money goes. Nor is he bothered by the fact that no one knows it comes from him. Brother Small's own words explain perfectly his attitude on this subject, he says, "I find great happiness in my relationship with God, and try to get closer to God everyday. I try to work for him. But, I can always feel him working in my life. In the most simple things I do, I can feel he is helping me. Nobody knows about most of the things I do at school, nobody knows about them. I like it that way. I like to do things like fix a window, when nobody knows it was me. But the Lord knows, and that's the most important thing to me."

Brother Small does many things that go unnoticed at Loyola. Fixing a broken window or picking up a ketchup-laden napkin may seem insignificant when compared to raising half a million dollars for the school. But to him they are no different. He does them both to serve God and to serve other people. As long as each and every one of his actions is motivated by God and love, Brother Small feels they are equally significant.

The thought that he is responsible for Patrick Martin's, or Melanie Selva's opportunity to be at Loyola never really crosses Brother Small's mind. Somewhere deep down he might know, maybe that is what motivates him. But, he never comes out and says, "Well, there are three kids here who wouldn't be if it weren't for me." He never mentions it. When he hears a story like Patrick's or Melanie's, he prays for the child, and for the family. He rejoices that the student has been able to attend Loyola. He does not however credit himself.

In addition to the money Brother Small makes from his commission and framing work, he generates a huge amount of money by selling his paintings at the school's spring fundraiser, the Ramble.

The Ramble is, to say the least, a huge production, a big party and an incredibly successful fundraiser. Each year the Ramble grosses approximately $600,000 and nets about $350,000 of that.

In May of every year, a veritable army of volunteers and paid workers descend on Loyola's gymnasium and decorate it in accordance with the Ramble theme for the year. The decorations are lavish; in fact they are so elaborate that they somehow completely mask the faded maroon and gold colors of the gym. The gym takes on a new identity for a night. In the past it has been the Wild West, a riverboat, or a summer soiree in the South of France. Whatever the decorations, the program remains the same each year: silent auctions, a gourmet dinner, a live auction, and a small breakfast for the guests.

There is an unimaginable amount of items for sale or auction at the Ramble: cars, tropical vacations, fine wines, jukeboxes, lawnmowers, autographed jerseys, helmets, and sneakers. Most guests probably never see all of it. But there is one area everyone visits: Brother Small's corner. One entire section of brick wall in the upper deck of the gym is reserved for Brother Small's one hundred or so paintings.

Recently his artwork has received some attention on national news, in the Chicago Tribune and in many of the local papers. As a result, his paintings have become more and more popular, and people have been willing to pay more and more for them. This is not to say, of course, that his paintings have not always been a big attraction at the Ramble. His paintings were a hit in 1969, when he first donated his art to the fundraiser. In that, the inaugural year of the Ramble, he donated a total of thirty-six different paintings to the party. Some of them were copies of Rockwell's, some were imitations of Monet's and there were even three originals.

A local wine distributor and Loyola Alum took a liking to Brother Small's paintings. He made a generous bid on all thirty-six of the paintings, but once he had made each bid, he pocketed the bid cards. Just minutes before the silent auction closed, he returned all of the cards.

At the end of the evening, he was the proud owner of the first thirty-six Jim Small paintings to be sold at the Loyola Ramble. Since then, the organizers of the Ramble have made a point to staple the bid cards to the tables. In fact, over the last four years the growing fervor surrounding Brother Small's artwork has prompted the director of the Ramble to station two Wilmette Policemen at his booth.

Brother Small has raised a huge amount of money by selling his paintings in the Ramble's live and silent auctions, though no one is quite sure how much. The most conservative estimates are around $200,000. Those who work closely with the Ramble estimate that the number is really somewhere between $300,000, and $400,000. No one has ever kept track of his earnings.

More impressive still, is the fact that he has raised even more money for the school through the sale of his commissioned paintings, frames and the donation of his salary. This year, all told he will give somewhere in the neighborhood of $100,000.00: $42,500 from his salary plus $35,000 from the Ramble, plus $15,000 for commissions and framing, plus another $10,000 in materials.

Brother Small's financial contribution is remarkable considering it comes from a guy who has not cashed a paycheck since 1952. It appears that Brother Small has nothing. Yet, in his career, he has managed to donate somewhere in the neighborhood of half a million dollars to Loyola. He's kept none of the money; so in reality he still has nothing. On paper, he is poor.

But, he has something, something so very special. He has his talent, his painting. But beyond that, he has a generous spirit. He has the inclination to take advantage of his gifts and utilize them to their fullest. He has the sight and the courage to live for others and not just for himself. He has the grace to love other people generously, without asking for any single thing in return. He will always have all of this. No one can take it from him. And as long as he has it, he will be rich, peaceful and happy.

Brother Small is back in his studio by 8:10 p.m. He usually paints until 8:30 and tonight will be no different, despite the fact that he just finished a frantic project. He walks into the studio, places a fresh canvas on the easel, and hangs a copy of Vincent Van Gogh's *Starry Night* in the same spot that Tim Ryan's poster had been hanging fifteen minutes earlier. He sits down behind the easel, picks up his palette, and reaches for a clean brush.

He squeezes some bright yellow paint onto the palette and methodically works his brush in and out of the thick oil paint. He reaches for the canvas and quickly crafts nine yellow circles, some large and some small. By tomorrow night these yellow circles will be the stars shining brightly on the city below in Van Gogh's celestial masterpiece.

Last spring, an audacious freshman named Elizabeth asked Brother Small if he would paint a copy of *Starry Night*.

"For you?" Brother Small asked somewhat amused.

"Well, no, not for me," she said, "for the Ramble, but I'll try to get my parents to buy it. They said they would, if you'd paint it."

"Sure, sure I can do that for you."

He kept to his word, and *Starry Night* was for sale the night of the Ramble. However, Elizabeth's parents, old friends of Brother Small's, did not place the highest bid; in fact, they were not even close. The painting was a big hit that night.

Now, seven months after Elizabeth initially asked Brother Small to do the painting, he sits down to do it again. This time it is not for the Ramble. It is for Elizabeth who will be turning sixteen next week.

Elizabeth's parents have been friends of Brother Small's for years. Their eldest children were some of his first art pupils, and since then he has become close with their family.

He paints for twenty more minutes. He has begun to augment the yellow ovals with bits of orange, and has even begun to surround it with blue in certain places. When he's done with his work at 8:35, Brother Small takes off his red magnifying glasses, and the purple shirt he has been wearing to paint and then dips his brush in the turpentine. He rinses it out in the sink near the door, working his fingers into the brush and forcing the paint into the sink.

He makes his way back to his room in the Jesuit residence. By 8:45 he has begun his evening prayer. This just might be the best part of his day. "I really look forward to my time for prayer," he says. "Maybe it's my age. But I really look forward to it, the same way I look forward to going to bed when it's cold and warming up underneath the covers." The first segment of his prayer is in the truest sense, preparation. He sits down at his desk and opens a small notebook to an empty page.

Then he sits back in the chair, closes his eyes and folds his hands in his lap. In a few minutes, he begins to write, but he only scribbles a few words on the paper. These words will be the points for his meditation tomorrow morning. He scribbles down two words: retreat dorm. The retreat dorm at Milford will be the first prelude for his prayer tomorrow morning. In this segment of the morning prayer, he will try to put himself in the presence of God. To do this, he usually picks some place where he feels close to God. Tonight he picks the dorm room where he stayed during his first Jesuit retreat

He scribbles down a long list of seemingly incomprehensible gibberish. Every morning, in the second prelude he prays for seventeen things. Many of the things on his list tonight are the same as the ones from this morning. But tomorrow he will pray that there may be peace on earth, and he will pray for the girls at Loyola who are finishing their Kairos retreat, the girls for whom he built the crosses.

Then he scribbles, "love God." After that he writes, "love gains more than understanding." After that, "love is grace." And finally, "only God can increase the grace." These four ideas make up the point upon which he will meditate tomorrow. This point is similar to the one from *Cloud of Unknowing* that he used in this morning's meditation, but this does not bother him because this idea is so very central to his life. His job is putting God's love into action, and to do this, he must know God's love, but more importantly he must love God, and want to do God's will. Understanding God is not nearly as important as loving God, and realizing and accepting God's love.

In the colloquy, the final segment of his morning prayer, he will again 'converse' with the Holy Trinity. Once he has finished making up the points for tomorrow's meditation, he gently slides off the edge of his chair and kneels before his desk. He always kneels for his afternoon and evening examination of conscience.

At first he lets his arms hang down in front of his body, and then he folds them, closes his eyes, and bows his head. Every night and every afternoon, he goes through the same routine prescribed by St. Ignatius for an examination of conscience.

What does he think about during the examination? I don't know, and he hesitates to say. What went right? What went wrong? Did his actions today spread love? Did his actions please God? Can he do better? Is he imitating Christ? Is he living a life worthy of God's love? It sure seems like it to me, but I don't know what he thinks about his day. I don't know if he is satisfied with how he lived today.

"Do you have goals for each day?"

"I think I have a goal insofar as I try to get better every day. That is my goal. Everybody shares the goal that they want to get better. For some people it means making more money or having more free time or spending more time with their family, but they all see it as getting better. I am just the same; I'm trying to get better each day. Each day I try to get closer to God, and I try to treat people better. The only way I can get closer to people, or to God, is by realizing that God put these people on the earth and then realizing that I'm not here just for myself. So if I can give a cup of cold water to a person on a hot day, I should. That would be good, and that's all I really want, to do good."

Looking at his life, I can't help but think how my life would be different if I had the discipline to sit down every night, even if only for a few minutes, and review my day. What did I do right? What did I do wrong? What made me happy today, and what made me sad? What would I have done differently? At the end of the day do I feel alive? Have I accomplished anything in the day? Have my actions impacted others in a positive or negative way? Can I live better?

But most nights I go straight to bed, worrying about the fact that I am getting to bed too late. I worry that I have too much to do tomorrow, and I also forgot to do something today. In all that rush, I fail to see God and I fail to see others. I only see me and my tasks.

If I would stop just for a moment and follow Brother Small's example, I might find that the busywork I have tomorrow and had today is not nearly as important as the relationships I have with God and the other people in my life. I would know that I shouldn't be quick with people. I'd remember how I didn't even look up from my computer while I carried on a conversation with my mom. I'd call someone, maybe my grandma, just to say hello. I'd remember to thank God, if for nothing else but the food I ate, the shower I took and the bed I will sleep in.

I don't stop though; I rush; and I'll probably rush more when I get up in the morning. But Brother Small does stop. Not only does he stop and look back at his day, he also looks forward and he sees so well. He finds the strengths and weaknesses in each day, and he uses these to prepare himself for the coming day.

When he completes his evening prayers, he leaves his room. He ends each day just as he began it, with a visit to the Blessed Sacrament. He walks down the same corridor. It's dark now like it was this morning. As he enters the chapel, he sees the blue light from the TV in the next room dancing against the wall in the dark silence of the empty corridor.

At the same time, Melanie Selva is wading through the third act of *King Lear* behind her desk in the Girls Hope house in Evanston. Tim Ryan has just given Lynne her painting, and they are embracing one another in the living room of their home in Winnetka. Patrick Martin is showering in the bathroom he uses at the McDermott's. Father Norm is sleeping fitfully amidst the drone of hospital machines and monitors.

When Brother Small enters the chapel, it is totally dark except for the red light burning over the wooden tabernacle that holds the Blessed Sacrament. He walks towards that corner of the room and kneels there before Christ's presence. The sounds from the TV next door occasionally come through the wall, but he does not seem to hear them.

He doesn't stay for long; in fact it's just a couple of minutes. He rises slowly and quietly and makes the sign of the cross by touching his right hand to his forehead, his stomach, his left breast and then his right breast.

He leaves without a word. Christ is the beginning and the end for him, everyday.

He walks back down the hall to his room.

As he enters his room for the last time today, he passes his reflection in the window. Once more, he does not even see it. He sees so much, but he does not see his reflection.

He goes to his room and prepares for bed. He takes off the frayed and faded sweater he has been wearing this evening and folds it, carefully putting it into the drawer on top of his other sweater.

His bed in the corner of the room is simple; there is one pillow with a white pillowcase and two brown blankets folded at the foot of the bed. It sits right under the window and, "It's perfect for sleeping," he says. He is in the bed by ten o' clock. Before he falls off to sleep he sees the light from the occasional passing car float for a moment across the ceiling of the room. In a few minutes, he is sleeping soundly. His left hand hangs limply off the side of the bed. The bandage for the cut on his hand fell off while he was painting, and the cut is bleeding ever so slightly.

Epilogue

Towards the end of the summer of 1997, Brother Small received word that he would be honored with a major award at the Loyola Academy President's dinner in November of that year. Receiving awards is nothing new for Brother Small who was chosen as the *1977 Educator of the Year: For Distinguished Professional Service at Loyola Academy.*

Not bad for a guy who has never taught a class at Loyola. Soon thereafter, in 1979, Brother Small was presented with the *President's Award: For Distinguished Leadership and Service to Loyola Academy.*

The awards continued. Sometime in the mid-eighties Brother Small was recognized as a *Loyola Academy Lifetime Founder.*

Nobody told him about this award, and he didn't even know his name was on the plaque until a friend of his who was visiting him more than a year later saw his name displayed and congratulated him. The Lifetime Founder Plaque commemorates those alumni and friends of Loyola who have contributed more than $100,000 to the school throughout their lifetimes.

Soon after his name was added to the Lifetime Founder Plaque, it was also placed on another plaque across the hall. The inscription on this plaque reads as follows,

Loyola Academy honors the members of its faculty and

staff who have ministered to this educational community
for twenty-five years or more. Their commitment, enthusiasm
and fidelity in forming young men in the Ignatian ideal
serve as an inspiration to their colleagues and the
young men (and women) of Loyola Academy.

Then in the fall of 1997, Loyola bestowed its highest honor upon Brother Small when they selected him as the recipient of the *Daniel A. Lord SJ Award: For Distinguished Service in the Cause of Youth.*

Fr. Lord is a perfect example of a man who truly lived the Ignatian ideal and many Jesuits consider him a hero. So, it is not surprising that they seriously consider the recipients for this award, which carries his name.

There were more people on hand to see Brother Small receive the Lord Award than there were to see Joseph Cardinal Bernadin receive his in 1989. There were more for Brother Small's dinner than there were for the famed Catholic author Mark Link in 1995 or for the French Cardinal Eugene Tisserant who received the Lord Award in 1964. There were even more people there to see Brother Small than there were to see the beautiful actress Loretta Young. Not bad for a guy who is "just a carpenter."

The funny thing is these awards don't seem to mean a thing to Brother Small. Rather he finds meaning in life in his relationships with God and with his numerous friends and family. The following are the words and thoughts of a few of the people whose lives he has touched.

Mary McCall, one of Brother Small's early art students is now a sophomore at the University of Virginia. She said, "I feel undeserving of his attention, for Brother Small is, honestly, an angel on earth. He is an inspiration to me. I love him and I am ever grateful for his friendship."

Margaret Kearney, another one of Brother Small's early art students, offered the following reflection: "Brother Small is nearly indescribable-he is the most generous man I have ever known. He is so willing to give of himself and his talents. He has been a mentor to me for as long as I can remember. I admire everything about him; he has taught me many important life lessons, like the meaning of friendship and the art of giving."

Sister Mary Paulina Small is 73 years old, four years younger than her older brother Jim. She is a retired Mercy Nun who volunteers her time acting as a one-woman welcoming committee at Mercy Hospital on the near south side of Chicago. She said this when asked to reflect on her brother: "The qualities that come to mind when I reflect on Jim's life would be: a man of deep faith, generosity and a keen sense of humor. On different occasions when I've been worried about something, he would always inject, 'Let the Lord take care of it.' He means so much to our family. We are proud of his gifts and thank God for his life. We are grateful that Brother Jim is our brother."

Lynne Fortunato, the proud mother of two Loyola graduates, met Brother Small in 1992. They became fast friends, and since then they have worked together year after year preparing the Ramble. Mrs. Fortunato said, "Brother Small has taught me over the years, with his consistent and unselfish compassion for others, to be more considerate and giving in my daily life. His love for other people is contagious. I love Brother Small; everyone does."

Marge McMahon, Brother Small's older sister, now lives in Oak Lawn, IL, just south of the city. She remarked, "When my 'little' brother Jim informed us that he was re-entering the Jesuits, selfishly I was downhearted about it. Besides being siblings, we were great companions. I always felt that Jim was the wind beneath my wings. But, after seeing how happy he was in his new life working and giving his talents to the Lord, I knew that God would give me the strength to fly alone, and that my little brother was 'small' in name only."

Stan Breitzman has been teaching physical education at Loyola for well over twenty years. He is very much a part of Loyola, and he has known Brother Small for much of this time. He said, "What I especially love about Brother Small is the feeling I get when I talk to him, in that God is a part of everything he does. His motive for everything seems to be that Jesus died for his sins and his method is following the Ten Commandments. Love and kindness for God are his living epitaph."

Kathy Shinkle has been coordinating the Ramble at Loyola for twenty years. Two years ago she found herself particularly moved by Brother Small's life and penned the following poem about him:

> What is a Brother Small?
> A person who listens with infinite patience and compassion
> to all of our joys and sorrows.
> A true "Brother Small" can make all our cares melt away
> with the touch of a hand or a smile.
> A Brother Small is never too busy to help anyone in need
> no matter how big or small the task may be.
> And with calm reassurance make everything brighter
> and make the day seem worthwhile.

Joe Gallagher and Jim Small grew up a few doors away from one another. As they grew older they grew closer. Their friendship was forged during the trials of the Depression, the excitement of childhood, the terrors of the Second World War, and the travails of failed romances when they returned home. Joe Gallagher said, "Brother Small is my best friend; he is the most caring and loyal person I know. The only small thing about him is his name. He is a tremendous man. Period."

Leigh and Isabelle Dunham are sisters from Wilmette, IL. They have been taking art lessons from Brother Small for the last two years. Leigh, a seventh grader at Wilmette Junior High commented: "Brother Small is a really nice man; he's the best art teacher I've ever had. I look up to him and he is the nicest man I know."

Leigh's little sister Isabelle, a six-year-old kindergartner from the Central School in Wilmette, added, "Brother Small is really nice, he teaches me about art. He's a special man because he picks out flower books for me. He's also really, really smart because he is OLD."

Brother Bill Haas and Brother Small have been great friends since the two of them joined the Jesuits forty-five years ago. They served together for years at Milford, West Baden and Loyola. They still make their retreats together and see each other at least once a week, though they are stationed in different places. Brother Bill said, "Brother Small knows and understands why God created him and why he called him to his vocation. He has always tried to serve others, no matter the inconvenience. He is one of the very best examples of a Jesuit, and he is a true and faithful friend to all, a man who is always trying to love and serve God and his neighbor more each day."

It's clear from these people's remarks that Brother Small has brought happiness to the world. He has made a difference, and he has without a doubt made the world a better place. By selflessly giving himself to God and to others, he has found happiness and peace in his life. In an earlier draft of the preface of this book, I said that he had achieved the ultimate goal, HAPPINESS. When he read this, he corrected me.

"Happiness is not the ultimate goal for me, serving God well is my ultimate goal, and I am pretty lucky because that kind of life makes me very happy."

He's been rewarded with award after award: he's had his name in print and on the screen. But these things are not the real rewards for him. Doing God's will is his reward. He knows that God is the only thing that can sustain him.

If someone showed up tomorrow and offered him a ten million-dollar check, he wouldn't change his life at all. He'd take the money; you bet he would! Then he'd fold the check up and put it in his pocket until he had time to stop at the treasurer's office. Then he'd slip it under the door and head back upstairs to do some more painting.

And the next day he'd be back at work in his cramped shop, which is wedged between a storage room and a boiler room in the dark basement of an aging school. And from those obscure quarters he would continue to bring his light to the world by doing the small things.

Works Cited

Allen, Paul. *Brother Jack, We need you here.* Chicago: Argus Communications, 1968.

Arrupe S.J., Pedro. *Studies in the Spirituality of Jesuits: Art and the Spirit of the Society of Jesus.* St. Louis: American Assistancy Seminar on Jesuit Spirituality, 1972.

Hopkins, Gerard Manley. "God's Grandeur." *Norton Anthology of Poetry: Third Edition.* Ed. Alexander W. Allison, Herbert Barrows, Caesar

R. Blake, Arthur J. Carr, Arthur M. Eastman, Hubert M. English, JR. New York: W.W. Norton & Company, 1983.

McBrien, Richard. *Catholicism: Volume Two.* Minneapolis: Winston Press, 1980.

Miller, Warren. "There are no Coincidences." *Chicken Soup for the Christian Soul.* Ed. Jack Canfield, Mark Victor Hansen, Patty Aubrey & Nancy Mitchell. Deerfield Beach, FL: Health Communications, Inc., 1997.

Saint Ignatius Loyola. *The autobiography of St. Ignatius.* New York: Harper & Row, Publishers, 1974.

Saint Teresa of Avila. *Daily Readings with Saint Teresa of Avila.* Springfield, IL: Templegate Publishers, 1985.

Printed in the United States
2646